Personal. Profound. Poignant. David tells a story like no one else; and these stories inspire reflection, hope and a genuine sense of connection.

Thank you, David. This book is what the world needs now.

— *Julie Winkle-Guilioni, International-Best Selling Author*

Essays of Hope, Healing, and Humanity

Tomorrow together

DAVID DYE

Tomorrow Together: Essays of Hope, Healing, and Humanity by David Dye

Published by Let's Grow Leaders LLC

PO Box 402 - PMB 227 Dillon, CO 80435

www.LetsGrowLeaders.com

Copyright © 2022 David Dye

Edited by Alexandra O'Connell
Proofed by Jennifer Jas
Cover, Illustrations, and Design by Mark Gelotte.com

ISBN: 978-1-7322647-4-8 (print)
        978-1-7322647-5-5 (ebook)

TABLE OF CONTENTS

DEDICATION

To our children – may we leave it better than we found it

ACKNOWLEDGMENTS

Tomorrow Together owes its existence to Matthew Candelaria for helping me find my way to the page. To Karin Hurt's love, support, and encouragement. To Sebastian Hurt for his reading recommendations. To Mark Gelotte for illustrations and cover design. And to my editor, Alexandra O'Connell, for her masterful ability to nurture writing (and the writer) from concept to completion.

I am grateful for you.

PRELUDE

I sat on the couch with my wife, Karin, and our teenager, Sebastian. We watched Lin-Manuel Miranda discuss the US Constitution through hip-hop music and rap lyrics, and ... I felt unease. The pandemic-caused isolation made the television release of Hamilton a big deal for us. We hadn't seen it live and were excited that Disney had made it available. It was a highlight in a summer of sameness.

Even if you haven't seen it, you probably know from the title that it follows the life of Alexander Hamilton and the many ways he influenced the founding of the United States of America. A song called "Non-Stop" describes how Hamilton conceived of The Federalist Papers to explain and defend the fledgling US Constitution to its new citizens. The song also tells how, despite writing with John Jay and James Madison, Hamilton ultimately wrote 60 percent of the essays himself.

The song highlights this volume of writing by asking why Hamilton writes likes he's running out of time? The question foreshadows Hamilton's death—a death everyone knows will arrive in a duel with Aaron Burr.

Why did he write like he was running out of time?

The lyrics hit me in the chest but differently than they were sung: Why wasn't I writing like I was running out of time?

If you knew me before picking up this book, that question might not make sense. Before this book, I've authored three books on leadership and management, a children's book, and hundreds of blog posts and articles. Books by Karin and me have been translated into Chinese and Turkish. Then there are the dozens more unpublished short stories and novels. It's fair to say I've written quite a bit.

But as I listened to Hamilton try to convince Burr to join him in writing The Federalist Papers, the words dug into my psyche. I was writing. But not like I was running out of time.

And I might be.

If the pandemic did nothing else, it sensitized many of us to our mortality. As I finish writing this book, we're living through what economists have dubbed the "Great Resignation." Forty percent or more of employees have left, or are considering leaving, their current job—either for another role, a different industry, a fresh start, or to retire.

There are many causes.

Some people felt ill-treated by their employers. Others found new life in their time with family during their work from home. And many people, faced with a once-in-a-lifetime global staring contest with mortality, realized they weren't living life the way they wanted to live it.

For me, those song lyrics set off a fuse of discontent. I love my work and my life. But I wasn't writing like I was running out of time—because if I were to write that way ... well, I would write *this* book.

INTRODUCTION

"The explorer who will not come back or send back his ships
to tell his tale is not an explorer, only an adventurer."
–Ursula K. Le Guin, *The Dispossessed*

A malaise, a frustration, a gloom hangs over our world. A feeling that we should be better than this. It is hard to imagine people not feeling this way during a (hopefully) once-in-a-century pandemic. But that question of why we can't prevent pandemic deaths–somewhere between ten-to-sixteen million people globally at the time of this writing, with nearly one million of those from here in the United States–is only one of many.

Why are our politics so polarized? How are we, once again, confronting the potential of nuclear war? Why can't we resist the divisiveness of social media, the interference by foreign actors, and the manipulation of our dopamine systems to sell advertising? How do we still live in a world where fear festers and basic human rights continue to be a struggle? John Philip Newell writes that we confront "A planet struggling to breathe, religious fundamentalisms that are fueling hatred and violence, and refugee families throughout the world being denied sanctuary."

That is a long, if partial, list of challenges for those who want to build a better world for themselves, their children, and their children's children.

These challenges can feel overwhelming. And hopeless.

But we're not without hope.

I've had occasional bouts of melancholy since I was a teenager. Melancholy is my word ... a non-medical diagnosis for what some might call occasional depression or anxiety. Despite that predisposition, I am optimistic. And perhaps I trust my optimism all the more because it is filtered through those times of cloying heavy gray.

I am hopeful.

But it is not naïve hope.

Pema Chodron writes that there "is wretchedness and gloriousness in being human, and they need each other. It is easy to get caught up in one and resist or yearn for the other." So easy to get caught up in either direction, yes. That resisting or yearning for one or the other is a form of naïve hope. But wisdom grows as we understand that we live with both aspects—as individuals and collectively.

I am hopeful because we have the wisdom and experience to work through our challenges. The challenges aren't easy. They will require new ways of thinking and new skills. Seth Godin suggests that modern citizens need to know about statistics, germ theory, epidemiology, decision-making, propaganda, the mechanics of global weather, network effects, and artificial intelligence. I'm sure you could add a few more to that list. We'll also need the flexibility to address unintended consequences. Patience, persistence, and determination.

One thing is certain. To succeed, we will need one another.

The good news is that we have one another. At least, we are available. We are here.

But there is real work ahead in lifting our gaze, extending our hand. Recognizing the dignity, beauty, wretchedness, and glory in one another. This work starts inside each of us.

Moving forward requires loving it all. To dance with what is wonderful—and what is painful. To know joy and sorrow in ourselves so we can embrace one another. To acknowledge the truths that even now we struggle to comprehend. We have one another. Need one another. But living into this truth requires effort.

Newell compares this dawning awareness to birthing pains. "There is no going back," he says. "We now know too much about the interrelatedness of all life to pretend that well-being can be sought for one part alone and not for the whole, for only one religion, one nation, one species." The work ahead is nothing less than to remember the sacred in one another.

And that is the goal of this book. To reconnect us to the beauty and pain of our humanity and the wisdom of the natural world that is our home. So that, together, we may build our better future.

If you've read our previous books, this one's different, and I believe it is an excellent companion. This is a collection of reflections, personal essays, delights, challenges, questions, and meditations. Hope, wisdom, and joy that equip one for life. Unlike our leadership books (Karin and I are known for our practical, easy-to-implement leadership tools and techniques), this book won't always provide clear answers. At times, a tough question is more important than an easy answer.

Each section focuses on a common theme. First up is Section I: A Together Future, where we look at the single planet we share and our opportunities to build the future, to face the challenges of communication, and to share the power of perspective. Section II: Connections focuses on what brings us together—from the connections of family traditions, good friends, and mentors to the kindness of strangers. In Section III: Embers and Hidden Treasures, I discuss the value of silence and sadness. Section IV: Follow the Music examines different approaches to wisdom, navigating life, and success. Section V: The Mountain Always Wins calls us back to humility and awe, the power of the world around us, and the importance of fundamentals. We end with Postlude: I Was Here, a celebration of our continued existence.

The sections are divided by interludes—I think of these as sorbets.

Palate cleansers. At least, I would think of them that way if I'd ever eaten a fancy multicourse meal that featured sorbets between courses. I haven't, but I can imagine. Each interlude is a kind of delight—a pause between themes. (And if you enjoy these interludes, I highly recommend *Delight* by J.B. Priestley and *The Book of Delights* by Ross Gay.) You may enjoy a chapter each day, a section, or more.

Everyone reads differently, but early readers of this collection were unified in one request: an orientation to my major life events. This is the sort of thing I would otherwise avoid (too much talking about myself), but I understand the need. You will find that I refer to various stages of my life in the pages that follow. These references aren't sequential. But like the map in the front of a fantasy novel, hopefully, this gives you context to enjoy the journey. So here it is:

I am the oldest of six children. I grew up in Denver, Colorado, with the Rocky Mountains only an hour's drive away. My family's economic status was working-class poor. My parents were usually employed, but we still relied on government assistance. This was the result of my parents belonging to a Christian-themed cult led by a man who'd come to the United States from India. He preferred his parishioners hold lower-income jobs as it kept them from realizing their self-sufficiency (and hence kept them dependent on him). My father was emotionally abusive, and during my elementary school years, my parents divorced.

I attended an academically advanced high school and then went to the University of Colorado in Boulder, where I ultimately majored in political science. During my freshman year of university, my father came out (told us he was gay) and left the family. I ended up caring for the oldest of my sisters while I finished my undergraduate degree.

When I was nineteen years old, I got involved in local politics and was appointed to the city planning commission. At twenty-one, I ran for city council and was elected to office. During that time, I started a master's degree in education. Before I started the student-teaching portion of the degree, I was recruited to join an educational human service nonprofit that worked with urban students—many of whom came from challenging situations, including poverty, drugs, and family violence. I accepted the position and worked there for sixteen years—most of that time spent in middle management and executive leadership roles. When I was twenty-four, I married for the first time. And while our marriage wouldn't last, one beautiful outcome was my relationship with my stepdaughter, Averie. She is one of the joys of my life.

During my years with the nonprofit, I re-engaged with my passion for leadership. I would eventually complete a master's degree in nonprofit management. I loved helping our leaders around the country be the best version of themselves. And so, I decided to do that exclusively. I retired from the organization I'd led and started my own leadership and management consultancy.

Soon after, I met Karin Hurt. In Karin, I found a kindred leadership spirit—we'd both written extensively, and our approach to leadership matched up so well that I thought I'd written an article I was reading ... until I saw her byline. Given our alignment, we decided to collaborate. We wrote *Winning Well: A Manager's Guide to Getting-Results without Losing Your Soul* and became good friends. We'd both been married before but were single at the time. After the book was published, we realized there could be more to our relationship than being friends and co-authors. We married, merged our businesses, and I became a stepparent for the second time (and I can say with confidence that I have the best children any stepparent could hope to have).

Together, Karin and I run an international leadership and management consultancy. It is amazing work to help leaders and organizations master the skills of human-centered leadership and achieve transformational results. This work has taken me around the world, and it inspires me. There is so much beautiful humanity in all of us— sometimes it's just knowing how to release it.

So, there's the context. If you'd like to learn more about our work, you'll find us at LetsGrowLeaders.com. I host the *Leadership without*

Losing Your Soul podcast and would love to connect there, on LinkedIn, or you can email me at david.dye@letsgrowleaders.com.

Here's to the journey!

SECTION I

A TOGETHER FUTURE

"The Earth is the only world known so far to harbor life. There is nowhere else, at least in the near future, to which our species could migrate. Visit, yes. Settle, not yet. Like it or not, for the moment the Earth is where we make our stand."
—Carl Sagan, *Pale Blue Dot: A Vision of the Human Future in Space*

I contend that Carl Sagan's *Pale Blue Dot* is the most important piece of writing in the twentieth century. The view of our planet taken from Voyager 1 as it neared the edge of the solar system is nothing more than a tiny dot of light. "Look again at that dot," he begins. "That's here. That's home." His description of all human history, of all known life, is haunting, humbling, and awe-inspiring. That dot, that "mote of dust suspended in a sunbeam" is all we have. That dot, and one another.

This section focuses on the future we can build together—all of us. Melba Pattillo Beals was one of the Little Rock Nine, the first nine Black students who registered to attend the formerly all-white Central High School in Little Rock, Arkansas. In her memoir *Warriors Don't Cry*, she writes, "The task that remains is to cope with our interdependence—to see ourselves reflected in every other human being and to respect and honor our differences."

Interdependence. It's one of those long words that means so much. John Green describes it easily: "All life is dependent upon other life, and the closer we consider what constitutes living, the harder life becomes to define."

In short, we need one another. The only real future we have is one that involves all of us.

But this is hard work.

When I held a local elected office, one of my assignments was to represent our city on a task force dedicated to four miles of road. At the time, those four miles of South Colorado Boulevard were the most heavily trafficked stretch of road in the state of Colorado. The task force included elected officials, real estate developers, school administrators, business chamber leaders, and people from every jurisdiction, department, or group with a stake in reducing traffic and making the road more usable for everyone. We considered many options, including localized mass transit, shuttles, lanes that could change directions, carpool clubs, ride shares (in the days before Uber/Lyft), metering, and more.

It was interesting work until I realized the group was doomed to fail. The realization happened one day when I heard one member emphasizing the need to reduce traffic because "it takes me thirty minutes to drive those four miles." The dozens of committee members nodded sympathetically.

Well, most of them nodded. I didn't nod because I couldn't empathize.

It wasn't because I was virtuous. I simply didn't own a car. I was still in college, supporting my sister, and was able to either walk, take public transit, or get a ride where I needed to go. My eco-friendly transportation wasn't virtue; it was economics. (As soon as I'd saved enough money, I bought my first car—a blue Dodge Colt.)

But as everyone nodded their sympathy at the frustrating gridlock, a light went on for me. I raised my hand and asked a question. "I'm curious," I said. "Who did not drive to today's meeting?" One person raised her hand. She was an elected representative who diligently tried to use the services she supported. The only other person who hadn't driven to the meeting was me—again, it wasn't virtue. The meeting was only three blocks from where I lived, so I'd walked there.

The group looked at me with curiosity. "Thank you," I said. "I ask because, as we've been discussing options, it seems like our goal is to get cars off the road." They nodded again but less patiently as I stated the obvious.

"Other people's cars ..." I continued. "We're trying to get *other* people to stop driving so that we can drive faster. Well, it seems to me that those other people will feel the same way. The only way any of this will work is if we create solutions that we would all use instead of our cars because they make more sense to us." The conversation petered out and eventually found its way back to the predetermined agenda items.

It was a good lesson for me. The only future that will work is one that we build together, for all of us. I recognize that defining what will "work" is challenging. We humans tend to consider ourselves unique and special. Different from those other people. But challenging or not, as Beals says, the task is to cope with our interdependence. Like it or not, for the moment, Earth is where we make our stand.

AN AGE OF MIRACLES

"There is no decency or sense in honoring one thing, or a few things and
then closing the list. The pine tree, the leopard,
the Platte River, and ourselves—we are at risk together,
or we are on our way to a sustainable world together.
We are each other's destiny."
—Mary Oliver, *Upstream*

We live in an age of miracles.

One morning, sitting in a restaurant in a Denver suburb, I had a
wonderful meal. Shredded beef short rib, seasoned perfectly, served
under an egg and covered by an excellent green chili. Music played
overhead—a soulful, bluesy piece by B.B. King. While I savored the
meal, I read a novel that I'd downloaded to my phone, paused to
arrange a Christmas purchase with my mom, and talked with my
daughter in Guatemala, my sisters, and Karin in Maryland—all via
text.

After breakfast, I popped into a drugstore and got an immuniza-
tion to prevent influenza. I replenished my travel kit with a toothbrush and razor before taking a beautiful, blustery walk in one of
my favorite Denver parks. Then I drove to the airport and boarded a
plane that, as I wrote this, carried me to Minnesota and North Dakota,

where I shared my expertise with people who need it. Then I visited a friend of many years.

Miracles.

Every one of my experiences on this day was once the exclusive experience of royalty or would have been viewed as devilish wizardry not so long ago. A meal assembled from spices gathered from around the world? World-class music played by one of the best? Near-instant communication with loved ones? A quick shot to prevent an illness that killed millions before we learned the power of vaccinations (something that seems even more miraculous these days)? Two hours of travel to make a trip that would have taken a week or two, weather permitting?

It's not just that these things exist. It's the people who make them happen.

How many people were involved in creating this single day? The number must be in the hundreds of thousands.

The people who grew the food I ate. Who cooked it. Who built the restaurant. Who engineered and built the electrical and natural gas systems that powered the restaurant. Who worked with King and recorded and distributed the music. Who researched immunizations. Who made the dose I received. Who brought it to that drugstore. Who built the roads, the airplanes, the airport. Who assembled my phone. Who built and maintain the network that transmits my texts. Who drew the oil from the ground that became the toothbrush and razor. Who manufactured them. Who built and run the system that allows me to insert a bank card and transfer value from my account to theirs. Who ... who ... who ...

The web of people responsible for one ... single ... day is nearly unfathomable.

Even more amazing ... nearly every one of those people responsible for my day had a choice. They didn't have to do what they did. They could have chosen to do something else or nothing at all. No one had to invent the thousands of inventions that made today what it is.

They chose to.

It's astounding, isn't it? Your life is the product of millions of decisions made by millions of people you will never meet. The monk Thich Nhat Hanh contended that "Without interdependence, nothing could exist." It's never been truer.

Your future is our future. We will build it together, imperfectly, in fits and starts, threatened always by our fears, insecurities, and the question of whether we can truly grasp our universal condition. We're all in the same boat—a boat called Earth.

DOWNTOWN

"If you're not careful / you'll up believing this is the world."
–Antonio Cisneros, *The Spider Hangs Too Far from the Ground*

I grew up in southwest Denver.

Late in the day, as the sun settled toward the mountains west of the city, I loved to see downtown Denver highlighted in the evening light. My favorite version of this view happened after a summer thunderstorm. The crenellated, steely-gray and white skyline glowed with hope against the dark-purple clouds that had taken their wrath out to the plains.

When I was twelve years old, my friend's mother invited us to volunteer with her at her job. We drove there on a cold December morning. We rode in the back of a pickup truck, lying down as flat as we could to stay out of the bitter wind. When we arrived, I sat up.

And the world shifted.

My skyline, the familiar arrangement of glass and steel, had been put into a cloth bag, shaken, and poured out. This was not my downtown. We were northeast of the city center, directly opposite of where I'd grown up. The buildings were foreign, strange, and discomfiting. Not at all the view I knew and trusted.

But then another thought hit me. There were children who grew up in *this* neighborhood. These alien buildings that discomfited me were their familiar anchors.

Recently, I shared this experience with one of my childhood friends, who told me, "By the time I was twelve, I'd lived with four different orientations of downtown Denver. I never had the same notion that it could have been a fixed point. That's a new perspective for me!"

There's always another perspective. The constellation Orion, with his starry belt and sword raised in the night sky for thousands of years, is a random smattering of stars to our neighbors at the other end of the galaxy. I've relived that moment of shifted perspective hundreds of times as my known world expands. There's always another perspective.

And as strange, unsettling, and foreign as it may seem—how important it is to remember that this is the only normal another person has ever known.

STANDING STILL

"From the quark to the supernova, the wonders do not cease.
It is our attentiveness that is in short supply, our ability and
willingness to do the work that awe requires."
–John Green, *The Anthropocene Reviewed*

What does it feel like to move at fifty-eight thousand miles per hour?

It turns out that we all know the answer.

Our sun, the star that science fiction authors often call "Sol" to distinguish it from other stars, moves through space at fifty-eight thousand miles per hour (93,342 kph).

That speed is hard to wrap my head around–but then I realize: the entire solar system orbiting the sun, all the planets and moons and asteroids, are also flying through space at fifty-eight thousand miles per hour as they stay in orbit around the sun.

Then there's our planet's movement to consider. Earth revolves around the sun. And it's moving fast, traveling around the sun at sixty-seven thousand miles per hour (107,826 kph). So, Earth covers just under one hundred million miles in one year.

Now, the Earth is also spinning. If you're standing on the equator, that's another one thousand miles per hour of rotation.

Let's put it all together: standing still on the equator, you're spinning at one thousand mph, traveling around the sun at sixty-seven thousand mph, in an entire solar system that's moving at fifty-eight thousand mph.

One thousand mph

Sixty-seven thousand mph

Fifty-eight thousand mph

And all that motion is pretty much impossible to sense. We only become aware of it if we pay enough attention over time.

It makes me wonder what else happens that we don't notice.

BUBBLES OF BELIEF

"We must listen and listen and listen. We must listen for the Truth
in our opponent, and we must acknowledge it. After we
have listened long enough, openly enough, and with the
desire to really hear, we may be given the opportunity to
speak our truth. We may even have the opportunity to be heard.
For no one and no one side is the sole repository of Truth.
But each of us has a spark of it within."

–Gene Knudsen Hoffman in *Quaker and Naturalist Too*
by Os Cresson

My father wanted to protect me from ideas that would challenge
the conservative spiritual beliefs I was raised with. Particularly in high
school, he tried inoculating me: "Nod your head and parrot back what
they tell you, but in your heart, hold on to the Truth." It was effective
(in the sense that it helped preserve some of those beliefs as I went
through high school). It was far less effective at helping me develop.
Self-reinforcing, isolating bubbles of belief may comfort us, but they
don't help us grow or become our full selves.

Fast forward two decades, and I'd grown out of that isolation. I
was once again in a classroom, not as a student this time, but as the

executive of a human service organization. I was talking with two of our teachers because I noticed they'd hung quotes throughout their classrooms from one religious tradition. Quotes from a variety of traditions could work with the content they taught, so I offered that as an option. "You can't hang quotes around your room from only one religious tradition. If you want to match the ones you've selected with thoughts from other traditions, go for it."

"But why would we do that?" they replied.

"Well," I said, "imagine that your child was attending school. They have a class with a dedicated, caring teacher who knows his subject well and is good at teaching it. He's also a committed Muslim, Hindu, Pagan, Buddhist, or Christian ... would you be comfortable with him filling his classroom with quotes only from his revered religious figures and teachers?"

"No, of course not."

"Then why would you do that to his children in your classroom?" I asked.

"It's different," they said, smiling and confident, "because we know that our way is the truth."

And there's the crux: "It's different because we know that our way is the truth."

Are there more dangerous words?

To assume the absolute correctness of one's beliefs ... that your way of understanding and thinking is perfectly aligned with objective reality ... is the height of arrogance. And yet so common.

How can we fear the Other? Because we know that "our way is the truth"—so their ways must be dangerous and wrong. Why do I need to learn more? I already know all the truth I need.

"It's different because we know that our way is the truth"—there's a failure of empathy here. Doesn't that dedicated teacher with their commitment to a different tradition believe the same?

And before we nod and condemn those close-minded Others, consider the truths that are so self-evident to you that you simply cannot believe how other people could be so [dumb, stubborn, naïve, misguided, sinful, lost] to see it differently. And recognize that those folks likely think of you and your beliefs in the same way.

I do not despair at these differences.

Influence is possible. We can learn from one another. Though it won't happen via internet memes. And definitely not by telling other people they are wrong, dangerous, or stupid for believing what they believe. That's never worked.

It begins with empathy. With being able to put ourselves in the other person's shoes and recognizing the Truth in their truth. If our ideas or beliefs cannot hold up to the scrutiny of competing ideas, perhaps they are not the truth we took them for.

I want to live in a world where people believe their way is the truth and can live and practice their truth but without preventing others from living theirs. I want that world. It is a world of astonishing beauty and variety. Of wonder and awe. Of constant learning and growth.

WILD DONKEYS

"There is nothing more deceptive than an obvious fact."
–Arthur Conan Doyle, "*The Boscombe Valley Mystery*"

Bonaire is a desert island in the south Caribbean that's known for fantastic coral reefs, flamingos, sea salt production, and donkeys. Coral, flamingos, and sea salt occur naturally in Bonaire. Donkeys–not so much.

In the 1600s, Spaniards brought donkeys to the island to haul salt and equipment. When more modern transportation became available, however, the people abandoned the donkeys to their own fate. The donkeys roamed the island, fending for themselves, without oversight or caretakers.

But Bonaire isn't the most hospitable environment for donkeys. Between the arid climate and increased tourism, many donkeys fell victim to illness and car accidents. They're also an invasive species and eat any moisture-laden plants they can find.

When Doyle has Sherlock Holmes tell us there's nothing more deceptive than an obvious fact, he could have been talking to me about Bonaire's donkeys. An invasive species that's suffering and harming the island's ecology? Wouldn't it make sense to solve this problem? Obviously! (At least it was obvious to me.)

That brings us to one solution: the Donkey Sanctuary. The sanctuary was started in 1993 to remove the animals from the incompatible environment and care for the sick, injured, and orphaned donkeys. Volunteers and donations helped care for the several hundred donkeys the sanctuary took in. Take care of injured donkeys, get them out of the wild, reduce their impact on the native plants and animals, and reduce donkey-human conflict. I visited the sanctuary, and it is a glorious, donkey-saturated time of smacking lips, crunching carrots, and wide smiles. Sounds like something everyone can get behind—obviously a good thing, right?

I thought so.

But it turns out that not everyone sees it the same way. A petition exists (supported by more than three thousand people out of the island's population of twenty thousand) to maintain Bonaire's wild donkey population. They argue that the sanctuary's practice of sterilizing male donkeys will eventually lead to the extinction of donkeys on the island. And for them, that's a problem.

Even though the wild donkeys aren't indigenous, their supporters view the donkeys as part of their culture and heritage for the past 450 years. They also have concerns about the humane treatment of donkeys within the sanctuary.

Their bottom line: they want the donkeys to remain wild and for people to treat them well.

Do you know this frustration? You figure out a great solution to an irritating problem and unveil it, only to find out that not only do people dislike your solution, but they also don't even see your problem as a problem. I've had this happen so many times: as a new supervisor trying to solve an "obvious" inefficiency in a process that my team had no interest in changing, and as a family member trying to better organize the kitchen.

In these moments, I'm always inclined to dig in, explain why I'm right, and try to "help" everyone else understand the facts that are so obvious to me. But you already know how that ends. As the saying goes, "Those convinced against their will are of the same opinion still." The Donkey Sanctuary situation made it clear: arguing is a waste of time and energy (though it does sell commercials for talk shows and "news" channels). But there is another way. We can listen.

When people can't see what's obvious to you, it's not that they're obstinate, ignorant, or broken. People are different. They've had different experiences, different values, and different personalities. They're looking at the world through all those filters—just like you do.

These are opportunities. To listen. To get their insights. To find out what is obvious to them. And to look for the "right" in their perspective. What is it that makes such obvious sense to them that they'll wonder how you could be so blind?

For myself, I'm a way better leader, parent, and partner when I stop coming to everyone with my answers, solutions, and my "obvious" facts. A tough question is more important than an easy answer. A discussion more valuable than a dictate.

Identify the issues that are obvious to everyone. Find the value in different perspectives. Then it's possible to find creative solutions that make far more sense and have more support than the limited but "obvious" approach.

It's not always possible to craft a solution that meets every need, but we'll never find it if we don't look for it.

A BETTER FUTURE

"The world is a huge cauldron and something big is cooking in it. We don't know what yet. Everything we do, feel, or think is an ingredient in that mixture ... What are we adding to the cauldron? Are we adding resentments, animosities, anger and violence? Or are we adding love and harmony?"
—Elif Shafak, *The Forty Rules of Love*

Indira is a spinal care specialist—the kind of doctor you would want to care for you if you were to suffer a major injury to your spine. She's exceptionally good at what she does. As a medical director and chief of spinal cord injury services, Indira has worked for decades to build creative and better patient-care solutions—which often means bringing disparate elements of the US health care system together to solve financial and clinical challenges.

As we became friends, Indira shared some of the behind-the-scenes challenges she'd faced in her medical leadership over the years. One head-scratcher involved convincing a hospital (and the other doctors) to prohibit smoking in the break room. Apparently, there was a permanent nicotine haze in the room as the surgeons and doctors enjoyed cigarettes between patients. "I mean, we're health care pro-fessionals, right? Am I the only one who sees a problem here?"

She prevailed.

One day, we were having coffee as Indira shared a new business project with me. She wanted advice about how to organize her thoughts, writing, and potential marketing for her new venture. Indira is a smart, accomplished, and courageous leader and doctor—but as we discussed this project, she seemed tentative. I explained that in some of the work she was doing, there wasn't a single "right" answer. That the best path for her could look different from mine or someone else's across town. Success would come as she took a step, watched how people responded, then adjusted, and took another step.

"Hmm," she mused, "that's hard."

I was surprised and said so. "I can see that you're tentative here. What makes this hard?"

She smiled at me—it was a patient smile. A smile I've learned to recognize as a long-suffering acknowledgment of my ignorance.

"David," she said, "I'm a Black woman. For my entire career, I've been the first Black woman the people around me have met in these contexts. First Black woman in medical school. First Black woman doctor. First Black woman hospital leader."

She paused to let me absorb that.

"At every step of the way," she continued, "many, if not most, of the people around me either expected me to fail or wanted me to." She said it without any bitterness—just a statement of fact with the same equanimity a surgeon might describe a traumatic injury.

"I had to be perfect so no one would ever have the opportunity to say, 'See—I knew she couldn't do it!' Getting it right at the highest level is my thing."

It's a story I've heard repeated many times from Black men and women in the United States. From Scott, the senior vice president of a global financial institution. From Mike, a human resource director. From Kwame, an educator. People actively working against you to undermine your success, or the assumption that you will fail because of the color of your skin—I'm not sure which would be worse. With active opposition, there is at least something to work against. But the

25

passive assumption that you won't make it is pernicious. The invisible attitude means lost opportunities—mentoring you never receive, openings you aren't considered for, or coaching that's never offered.

And I've never experienced any of it, nor will I.

As the United States and the world reckon with the ugly truths of how people have treated one another, one thing I'm confident of is that you can't heal without acknowledging the injury. My life has had its challenges, yes, but as a white man in the US, I didn't grow up with many of my teachers subconsciously assuming my failure. I was able to look at television and movies and see a wide range of people like me doing all kinds of amazing things. I've never been profiled or assumed guilty because of my skin color. Never been denied a loan, a home, or a job.

In writing this book, I thought about one of the activities I enjoy when I travel and have a little extra time: getting lost. Taking a walk or a run and twisting and turning until I'm not quite sure where I am, then exploring the new city, town, or countryside until I figure out where I am. It's a fun way to get to know a place. I've done it for decades—and only once have I felt uncomfortable (a region in northern California that I later found out was known for its illegal marijuana). I took for granted that I can jog just about anywhere I feel like it, without concern. Ahmaud Arbery couldn't jog where he wanted.

You can't heal without acknowledging the injury. That's true for broken bones, major cuts, or internal trauma—and if you're reading this and you're a white person living in the United States, then you, like me, have had advantages in your life that have nothing to do with your talent, skill, or hard work. That doesn't mean your life hasn't been hard. It doesn't mean you haven't had a share of injustice. And it doesn't mean you haven't worked hard to do what you've done. It's not something to feel ashamed or guilty about. Acknowledging it gives those of us for whom it's true the power to help build a better future—for all of us.

SUIT UP

"People who wade into discomfort and vulnerability and tell the truth
about their stories are the real badasses."
-Brené Brown, *Rising Strong*

There's something about a uniform.

Put on your running shorts and shoes, and your body goes into run mode. Watch Naval Academy midshipmen accompany their mothers through the streets of Annapolis in their dress whites, and you probably stand up a little taller. Put on a hard hat, orange vest, work pants, and boots, and you can walk into moving traffic, tell it to stop, turn this way or that—and they'll do it.

When I joined the debate team in high school, I quickly realized that there was a uniform. For the students from rich schools, it was a navy blazer, khaki pants, and a conservative tie for the boys; business suit-dresses for the girls. For those of us who were less well-off, it was whatever slacks, dress shirt, sweater, tie, or blouse/skirt combo you could assemble.

But not Robert. Robert was a classmate who had started debate a year before I did. I looked up to him (literally—he was two inches taller than me, but he was also successful). He taught me how to research, how to construct arguments, and to build a portable library of quotes written on index cards. Robert was charismatic, and from the time I met him, he wore a suit to every debate tournament.

How I envied him in those suits.

He had a gray one and a black one, sophisticated, and they lent unconscious ease and gravity to any argument Robert made. I'm not saying he won tournaments because of those suits. But it didn't hurt.

And I had to get one.

I mowed lawns, cleaned gas stations, and did whatever other odd jobs I could find to save for a suit of my own. As our junior year started, I returned for the fall season rocking a new charcoal-gray suit. And I had a flowery blue tie. None of those blazers and conservative ties for me. I might not have had two suits like Robert, but I was determined to make the one I did have do full duty.

Robert and I would go on to win many tournaments and compete at the national tournament. We finished in the top twenty in the country (Robert one spot ahead of me) our senior year. I'm not saying it was because of the suits—but they didn't hurt.

Today, Robert has a successful career as an attorney and professor of law. As he was approaching his fortieth birthday, he shared this reflection on Facebook.

> My freshman year in high school, I joined the debate team. I had been winning oratorical competitions since second grade, so it seemed like a natural fit. In my first competition, which was a large invitational tournament hosted by my high school I went undefeated. However, I had not expected to do so well. So, I wore what I thought would be appropriate attire, a nice sweater, slacks (with sort of an athletic look), Jordan's, and a gold rope chain—and I went onstage and collected my trophy in front of hundreds of competitors.)
>
> Afterwards, my ever-patient debate coach told me to go buy a couple of suits for the tournament the next week, as my attire would affect perceptions of me. I told her that a purchase of a couple of suits wasn't really in the family

budget. We went to a thrift store and bought a black suit and a grey suit that I wore for several years to debate competitions.

Although I did extremely well at high school debate, winning many tournaments including the State Championship my Senior Year and qualifying and advancing at Nationals twice, I always thought about the disadvantage I had in not having more money to spend, as compared to my suburban counterparts.

They would purchase boxes of evidence, whereas I would go to the Public Library (or the University of Denver) and would write down quotes on note cards—to avoid the expense of copying pages—as evidence. They would buy canned arguments, whereas I would painstakingly write every word out. And most notably, and universally, they always wore the same J. Crew Blue blazer, white shirt, striped tie and khakis to every tournament. I wore someone else's old donated wool suit.

Yet the insecurity of those two old wool suits served me well in debate and life. Hours spent in college libraries researching (to overcome what I perceived was the disadvantage of coming from an urban school, being the only Black male many judges and competitors ever saw doing debate, and the lack of resources) turned out to hone skills in research that were great benefits to me as a young associate at a large law firm. Knowing how to find the answer for yourself, after spending years as a high school student doing that and competing against folks reciting briefs prepared by college students, helped greatly as a young lawyer—when I could afford to buy my own suits.

I thought of those suits as uniforms for work. I put it on just like my high school track uniform and sports uniforms since. But what I thought was a disadvantage then, turned about to be an advantage later in life.

It's hard to describe how humbling and meaningful it was to discover the experience of Robert's suits from his point of view. You can forgive two high school students, each with their own insecurities, for not discussing their clothes. But how often in life do we needlessly compare ourselves, completely unaware of the full story?

Thank you, Robert, for the gifts of your example then and your perspective now.

TAKE THE CASH

"To attain knowledge, add things every day.
To attain wisdom, remove things every day."
–Lao Tzu

My father had a saying: "Take the cash and let the credit go."

It sounds like advice from a bank robber, right?

I remember the first time he told me to take the cash: I needed to learn how to draw a bicycle for a project, but I was not (am still not) a visual artist. I asked my older friends if anyone knew someone who could help. They pointed me to a man living three miles away. I called and made an appointment, and my father took me to meet him. It turned out this man was quite skilled and often taught young people to draw. In thirty minutes, he helped me draw a reasonable bicycle.

Walking through his house, we passed by the most amazing home bar. Fancy colored bottles of every size and shape sat on shelves in front of a large mirror. Decorative lighting made the bottles sparkle. I'd never seen anything like it. He also smelled strange and had a very red face.

I'd just met my first alcoholic.

When I was growing up, there was no alcohol in our home, nor in the homes of any of our friends from church. Up to that point in life, I'd never even seen someone drink a beer or glass of wine in person. That was something people did in movies. I didn't know much about alcohol except that it was one of a long list of things that God clearly didn't approve of.

But I didn't feel judgmental about this art teacher's bar—it was beautiful.

Once we'd left his house and returned to our car, I commented on that amazing collection of colorful bottles. My father turned to me, one arm slung across the steering wheel, and said, "When it comes to people, you've got to take the cash and let the credit go."

I understood his words as an admonition: appreciate the man's art and teaching, but don't become a drunk. Oh, and forget about the colorful bottles; they'll only get you in trouble. He didn't say any of that, but my father excelled at subtext.

Many years later, I got curious about his advice. It didn't sound like something he'd make up. So where did it come from? And why the hostility toward credit? Turns out, it's a line from a nineteenth century translation of Persian poetry, the *Rubaiyat of Omar Khayyam*. Here it is in context:

> Some for the Glories of This World; and some
> Sigh for the Prophet's Paradise to come;
> Ah, take the Cash, and let the Credit go,
> Nor heed the rumble of a distant Drum!

And the funny part is that it doesn't mean at all what my father intended. It's a call to enjoy today and don't worry about the future. Carpe diem, but more hedonistic. Totally not what he had in mind.

PEOPLE AND TREES

"But can you tell me where he gets his whiskey?"
–Abraham Lincoln (or maybe not)

In 1863, the *New York Herald* published this story regarding President Lincoln's response to criticism of General Grant:

> A committee of abolition war managers waited upon the President and demanded the General's removal, on the false charge that he was a whiskey drinker and little better than a common drunkard. "Ah!" exclaimed Honest Old Abe, "You surprise me, gentlemen. But can you tell me where he gets his whiskey?" "We cannot, Mr. President. But why do you desire to know?" "Because, if I can only find out, I will send a barrel of this wonderful whiskey to every general in the army."

No one's quite sure if Lincoln actually said this. And if he did, it's likely he took inspiration from others before him who had said similar things. My favorite of these might be King George II. An advisor criticized one of the king's military appointments, saying he was unfit for the role because he was a madman. The king responded that he hoped his appointee would bite some of his other generals to transmit the madness.

In Washington, D.C., just seven miles away from the Lincoln Memorial (where there is no mention of General Grant's whiskey) is another national treasure: the United States National Arboretum. Winding roads and trails take you through groves of holly and magnolia trees, Japanese woodlands, incredible azaleas, dogwoods, a grove of every state tree, and a panoramic view of the Anacostia River. It's one of my favorite places in the District.

But of all the wonders in the arboretum, my favorite is the National Bonsai Museum. It's home to more than three hundred of the most incredible bonsai trees I've ever seen. And at the heart of this collection is my favorite tree. Not just my favorite in the collection—my favorite tree. It's a nearly four-hundred-year-old Japanese pine.

One time I visited the museum in mid-July when it was 98 degrees and raining. Despite the rain, I paused when I arrived at this Japanese pine. Standing there taking in the magnitude of this tree, I felt my tears begin to blend with the rain.

To understand why a tree could produce such deep emotions, it helps to understand a little about bonsai. The trees grow in pots, and both branches and roots are regularly pruned, trimmed, and guided. As a result, bonsai trees can require near-daily care to survive. To see this tree is to see the many generations of Japanese families that cared for this beautiful work of living art for centuries. It's a testament to human creativity and discipline.

But it's more than that. In August 1945, this tree and the family that cared for it survived the atomic bombing of Hiroshima. Thirty years later, it was gifted to the United States by Japan during the US bicentennial celebration.

The artistry and history are overwhelming.

The first time I visited the Bonsai Museum, I asked one of the gardeners, "How do you make these trees so beautiful?"

He cocked his head, squinted one eye, and said, "Son, you don't make a tree do anything."

He continued, "That's not our job. Bonsai isn't about making a tree beautiful. You care for the tree, find the beauty and strength it already has, and reveal that."

I think the bonsai gardener would have got along well with Lincoln or King George (though without the biting). People are a lot like trees. You can't make a tree do something—and the same holds true for people.

There is peace and joy in appreciating people for who they are. To see their beauty and strength. To enjoy and celebrate each person's unique energy, talents, personality, skills, interests, and abilities—all that they add to the world and to your life.

And, unless it's truly toxic or harmful, let the rest go.

HOW CAN WE LIVE

"If only it were all so simple! If only there were evil people somewhere insidiously committing evil deeds, and it were necessary
only to separate them from the rest of us and destroy them.
But the line dividing good and evil cuts through the heart of every
human being. And who is willing to destroy a piece of his own heart?"

—Aleksandr Solzhenitsyn, *The Gulag Archipelago*

The fundamental question of our time is this: How can we live together?

How can ...

We who believe life results from a creator live alongside we who believe life is a fragile miracle of chance?

We who believe our way is the only way live alongside we who believe there are many ways?

We who believe in freedom and responsibility live alongside we who believe in security and protection?

We who believe in questioning a way of life built on injustice and treachery live alongside we who believe you cannot change the past and the race goes to those who hustle?

We who believe in the common good live alongside we who believe in the good of the individual?

We who believe in sharing and preservation live alongside we who believe in taking what you can get before someone can take it first?

We who believe our God is more real and more powerful live alongside we who believe our God is more real and more powerful live alongside we who believe our God is more real and more powerful live alongside we who do not believe?

We who believe that health care is a basic right live alongside we who believe you get the health care you can afford?

We who believe that who you love is a matter of your own heart live alongside we who believe that who you love threatens our communities?

We who believe you should sell to or serve everyone live alongside we who believe conscience dictates that you sell to or serve those who believe as us?

We who believe your resources belong to us live alongside we who believe your resources belong to you live alongside we who believe your resources don't belong to anyone?

We who embrace love live alongside we who guard against it?

We who want to build a future live alongside we who want to bring an end?

We who hurry live alongside we who tarry?

We who hunger live alongside we who feast?

We who hope live alongside we who fear?

We who laugh live alongside we who weep?

We who live live alongside we who die?

We who believe live alongside we who do not?

We share a very small rock, after all.

Or, at least, we all call it home. Whether we will find a way to share it remains to be seen.

How can we live together?

INTERLUDE I

MORNING COMFORTS

"Would you like an adventure now,
or would you like to have your tea first?"
–J.M. Barrie, *Peter Pan*

The morning has a series of delights all its own.

I love to slip my feet into my sandals. That's always a good start to the day. The soft feel of your favorite pajamas or worn shirt in the morning. The warmth from a mug of tea. The smell of morning food.

I was listening to a Vietnamese chef describing the joy of waking up on Sunday mornings to the smell of his grandmother's *pho* filling the house, and how much he enjoyed those first warm slurps. Whether it's pho, chili and eggs, bacon, coffee, pastries, or fresh-baked bread, the smell of delicious food waiting for you is one of life's joys. It's been several years since I camped outdoors, but when I did, this was a delight I loved to share. To ease people's transition to waking by enticing them out of their tents with fresh coffee and sizzling bacon and the smoky warmth of a small wood fire.

Perhaps morning delights are so delightful because you must earn them by getting out of bed. I've never found the transition from sleep to wakefulness to be pleasant. Sometimes it is jarring (too little sleep and too loud an alarm). Other times it is a slipping away from dreams to consciousness. Either way, you've got to get out of bed–and that's obviously why God invented bladders.

When I was in grade school and my father was between steady jobs, he delivered newspapers. I would wake up at 4 a.m. to help fold, rubber band, and place the newspapers on customers' porches. (We were placers, never throwers.)

What I remember most about delivering those early morning newspapers are the smells. As you begin, almost no one is awake, and the morning air is the most fresh and crisp it will be before cars and trucks add their exhaust. As you walk from house to house, setting papers on the porches, you can smell the houses that wake early. Often it was a mix of someone's first cigarette and black coffee. There were houses where homemade tortillas mingled with the lingering smokiness of chili peppers. I have always wondered how a house could have a distinct smell that you could discern from the porch or sidewalk outside, but they do.

My favorite-smelling house had white siding and a faded clay sun sculpture hanging on the porch. On weekdays, it was quiet and neutral, but on weekends, the kitchen light was on and the delicious smell of pancakes or waffles and bacon flowed through the windows and door frames.

As the dark turned to purple pre-dawn, we would deliver our last newspapers to a few blocks of close-packed little square houses just behind a grocery store. The store's giant exhaust fans filled the little neighborhood with the aroma of the new day's baking bread and doughnuts. Decades later, I can still take a deep, satisfied breath of that tantalizing, sweet, yeasty reward for another day's papers delivered.

SECTION II

CONNECTIONS

"There are no individuals. There aren't even separate species.
Everything in the forest is the forest."
—Richard Powers, *The Overstory*

Where do you go when you first travel to a famous place?

I'd been invited to San Francisco to deliver a keynote presentation at a conference. This would be my first time in the city by the bay, so I added a day to my trip: I had to see California's coast redwood forest. It's not every day you get to see the world's tallest living thing, and I didn't want to miss the chance (and yes, I checked out that famous bridge too).

The redwoods did not disappoint. If anything, they were more impressive in person than in my *Return of the Jedi*-speeder-bike-fueled imagination. Some of them are thousands of years old. Try to fathom what that means. Not one hundred years old—that just gets you back to the first days of the automobile. One thousand years is a long time. They are all tall, but some of the trees are immense. I spent time with the tallest tree—as tall as a thirty-six-story building, with a trunk that would take ten or twelve people to encircle.

There used to be so many more of these trees. I am glad these survive, but people cut down 95 percent of the redwood forests. As I walked the soft forest floor, my awe and humility before these incredible living things mixed with sadness for what we've lost—what we took from ourselves, our children, and the world.

My contemplation soon gave way to curiosity. Throughout the forest, there are occasional trees that had fallen over. Standing next to a fallen tree trunk that is wider than you are tall is an experience—but that's not what made me curious.

It was the roots.

I expected these forest giants to have equally immense roots that plunged deep into the earth. But what I saw were relatively shallow holes where the root ball tore out of the ground. There were no jagged ends to suggest giant roots had been left behind. It was strange.

When I returned to my hotel that night, I went online to see what I could learn about the redwoods' roots. What I found surprised me.

I expected the redwoods to have deep root systems, but they don't. Their roots only go down five or six feet ... but they extend outward a hundred feet. In fact, the roots of nearby trees entangle, connect, and even fuse with one another. Together, the trees anchor one another through thousands of years of storms, winds, and floods.

The tallest living things on Earth don't grow tall by themselves.

They do it together.

In this section, you'll find reflections on our most valuable connections, what it means to be connected, friends, and the challenges of communication.

Who are your connections?

As I consider the roots that hold me up through storms, I also wonder: How am I supporting them?

A CRAB PROVIDES
LITTLE FOOD

"A crab provides little food, so he is not easy to eat.
But the little he does offer is the best food under the sky.
To eat crab you must work, which makes you appreciate
him more. He is the blessing, the remembrance.
And no man or woman ever ate enough."
—James Michener, *Chesapeake*

Growing up in the Rocky Mountain West, I was ignorant of crabs. I'd never eaten one, and it was hard to imagine why you'd want to. I first became aware that crabs are a "big deal" when I went to grad school.

In a social marketing class, we studied how to positively affect human behavior on a large scale. It was a fascinating look at humanity. For instance, an anti-littering effort in Texas didn't take off until they figured out two key elements: the right slogan and the right faces. The prime littering population was young men aged sixteen to twenty-four ... in a state known for its swagger and independence. So, a call to public responsibility was unlikely to work.

A marketing agency came up with the right slogan: "Don't mess with Texas." Yes, "Don't mess with Texas" got its start as an anti-littering campaign (the Texas Department of Transportation owns the trademark). Then they put it in the mouths of Texas celebrities: rocker Stevie Ray Vaughan and Dallas Cowboys football players Randy White and Ed "Too Tall" Jones. The combination of slogan and celebrities worked: in four years, roadway litter declined 74 percent.

Back to the crabs and the Chesapeake Bay where, by the early 2000s, years of public education had reduced pollution from agriculture and sewage treatment. But there was still too much nitrogen and phosphorous flowing into the Bay. These nutrients spiked algae growth, which blocked out the sun for plants lower in the water. Then the algae died and decomposed, sucking oxygen out of the water. None of this is good for the marine life (or seafood, if you prefer).

Studies identified fertilizer runoff from residential lawn care as a major source of this pollution. It was time for another social marketing campaign. But the past forty years had featured hundreds of "Save the Bay" efforts, and the folks working to reduce pollution knew people would be tired of those messages.

Enter the blue crab.

Rather than focus on another environmental cause, the marketers appealed to regional pride and love of the crab with messages like "Save the crabs—then eat them" and my personal favorite: a photo of a house with lush green grass beneath which is printed "No appetizers were injured in the making of this lawn."

I remember studying this campaign and being struck by how an appeal to eating crabs could change behavior at scale. In my mind (and at the risk of rejection by my East Coast family and friends), that would have been like trying to persuade Westerners to drive less so they could eat more Rocky Mountain oysters.

Like I said, I was ignorant.

How could an ugly crustacean inspire that level of loyalty? It would be years before I understood.

Karin was born and raised in Maryland between Baltimore and Washington, D.C. When she introduced me to her extended family, it was at a crab feast. When her nephew brought his girlfriend to meet us, it was at a crab feast. If I was clueless about crabs in general, I knew even less about a crab feast. Apparently, they are a sort of gauntlet where you test romantic partners to see if they are worthy.

The first thing you need to know is that you hold your crab feast outdoors if at all possible. Set up folding tables end-to-end, roll out brown butcher paper or newspapers across the surface, tear it off, and use masking tape to hold it to the table for an inexpensive and disposable tablecloth. Place rolls of paper towels on the table every few feet, such that everyone has a roll within arm's reach.

Family and friends arrive with an abundance of side dishes—of which salads, boiled corn, and mac and cheese seem to be particularly important, though I imagine this varies by family tradition. Distribute wooden mallets and knives around the tables (two or three house-holds often pool their mallets so there are enough for everyone). Add a generous supply of soft drinks and beer (nothing too fancy—the consensus seems to be that craft beer is wasted at a crab feast) in a cooler, bucket, or tub of ice.

Everyone takes their seat, and now it's time: bushels of bright red steamed crabs are dumped in the center of each table (the crabs come out of the water with blue markings on their legs and claws—hence the name—but once steamed, like lobster, they turn a bright red).

The crabs are even more red due to the speckles and clumps of Old Bay seasoning—a remarkably spicy, salty, not-quite-sweet flavor combination of salt, celery seed, dry mustard powder, red pepper, black pepper, bay leaves, paprika, cloves, allspice, ginger, cardamom, and cinnamon that you don't want to get in your eyes. But seasoning is a misnomer. Seasoning implies restraint—a little spice to draw out the flavor. Not so with crabs. You pour it in by the bucketful. If you can see the crabs beneath the layer of seasoning, you almost have enough.

48

Now for the drama.

Opening a crab and removing the meat is known as "picking." And apparently, there is a right way to pick a crab.

But I couldn't tell you what it is. Nor, I'm guessing, could three different Marylanders. Legs first or body first? Legs connected to the body or not? Everyone seems to have their preference.

But there does seem to be universal agreement on this point: thou shalt not waste crab meat.

The kindest of grandmothers can summon wrath to cower a Navy SEAL when a grandchild discards an errant leg with useable meat attached. As she picks the leg, Nana ruefully shakes her head at her adult child whose parenting produced such waste. "I raised you better than that."

Children born in states that don't directly border the Chesapeake are granted a little more grace. A little more.

Before meeting the crabs and Karin's extended family, I watched several crab-picking instructional videos. After which, Karin told me that they would have shown me the ropes and that I was overthinking it. I'm not so sure—the stakes felt high.

Fortunately, I did not completely embarrass her—though there is a family photo of her father holding up a large piece of crab meat for my examination with an expression that requires no interpretation: "Now that's how you pick a crab!"

And with the picking of the crabs and the pounding of the mallets and the licking of the fingers rubbed raw with crab shells and the sting of seasoning comes the conversation. The relaxed catching up of careers, holidays, celebrations, illnesses, children who are older than they ought to be, laughter, plans, and thoughts for those who cannot be there.

And I get it. Michener was right: "A crab provides little food, so he is not easy to eat. But the little he does offer is the best food under the sky."

The crab isn't the best food because it is delicious (though it is), nor does it tick every culinary box. It is the best precisely because it is not easy to eat. You cannot rush through picking crabs. You cannot scroll social media while picking crabs.

Crabs are time. With family. With friends. For connection. The crab is the blessing, the remembrance–and certainly worth changing your lawn fertilizing routine.

So you can save them, then eat them.

A GOOD MIRROR

"It is the obvious which is so difficult to see most of the time.
People say 'It's as plain as the nose on your face.'
But how much of the nose on your face can you see,
unless someone holds a mirror up to you?"
–Isaac Asimov, I, *Robot*

Who are the friends who water the dusty ground of your soul when you need it?

After nearly a year of pandemic-enforced isolation from everyone but immediate family, I'd hit a wall. Together with Karin and Sebastian, our then-fifteen-year-old, we'd weathered the lockdowns, masks, and physical distancing as well as one could hope. Which is to say, we still loved each other and were beyond ready to see someone else in person. Anyone else. (And our hearts broke for people who've endured the pandemic living alone.)

Despite having a rock star family and the ability to work from home with clients around the world, my mental health took a beating, and many others experienced this too. I know I'm not alone here–everyone had their own struggles, heartbreaks, frustrations, and epiphanies through this journey. And it's important to note that (at the time of this writing) in many parts of the world, this will continue to be the case for at least another year or two.

On a late winter day when warm winds made it pleasant to spend an early afternoon outside, I was able to meet a close friend for a beer, a few hands of cards, and conversation we hadn't enjoyed in a long while. In the absence of personal friends, my psyche felt brittle. Like a houseplant that has gone without water too long, leaves still clung to their stems, but if you were to shake the plant, they would fall to the floor. Or perhaps like a balloon filled near to bursting with unspoken angst, frustration, questions, self-measuring, and self-loathing.

We talked and talked, my words tumbling out with hardly a breath between, halting, searching through feelings until ... aha, there it is. The crux of what's bothering me. The pea beneath the mattress. A kind of pain that must be discovered and exposed to air to heal.

Conversation with an old friend is spring cleaning for the soul. Throw open the windows and see yourself more clearly, reflected in the perspective of another person you can trust.

Living your life with no mirror is challenging. While we know ourselves well from the inside, without a good version of Asimov's mirror, we can't even see our nose. Our image is incomplete, fuzzy, or even warped. All of us, moving through life as we do with our own experiences and values, are imperfect mirrors for one another—vital but insufficient. Old friends who know us well sharpen the focus, and good friends bring high-definition clarity to their reflections.

Which prompts me to ask: How can I be a better mirror and a better friend?

How can we improve our ability to reflect back others' beauty, strength, dignity, joy, sorrow, and struggles in a way that makes them more perfectly ... them?

CAN I ASK A FAVOR?

"To love someone is to learn the song in their heart and
sing it to them when they have forgotten."
–Arne Garborg

I'd like to ask a favor.

It won't take long, and I'm sure it will mean the world to someone—and I know I'd be grateful. I'd like to ask you to send a quick email
to a woman named Mary. But first, let me explain …

I published my first book, *The Seven Things Your Team Needs to
Hear You Say*, in 2013. Before that, I'd written quite a bit, but that was
the first book I published. That summer, as is often the case for new
writers, I was bogged down, unsure of the process, concerned about
the value of the words I'd put to paper, wondering how—or even if—to
take the next steps.

Mary Kelly, PhD, CSP, CDR, US Navy Ret., is a force of nature. She
has a PhD in Economics, a storied career in naval intelligence (well,
I'm certain there are stories—she just can't share any of the good
ones), and an ebullient love of wine, dogs, and people (in that order,
though it might be a toss-up between wine and dogs). I'd gotten to
know Mary through our membership in the National Speakers Asso-

ciation. We attended a conference together, and on the return flight, I sat next to her. During our conversation, she asked me how my book was coming along.

When I expressed hesitation, the smile left her face and Commander Kelly made an appearance. With steely eye contact, she said, "David, you're going to finish that book."

"Yes, ma'am," I replied, "the thing is, I'm just not sure how—"

"Look," she cut me off, "here's what you do ..."

And for the next thirty minutes, Mary gave me a crash course on exactly how I could complete the book and have it ready for a conference planner who wanted a copy for all her attendees.

I made the deadline. In gratitude for her encouragement, I sent Mary the first signed copy. A few weeks later, we ran into each other. She greeted me with a hug and a big smile. "David, I read your book."

I waited for the inevitable feedback. Mary isn't one to mince words.

"Oh. My. God. David, you are a good writer."

I smiled. "Thank you, Mary."

"No," she said, the smile once again leaving her face. "David, I'm serious, you are an incredible writer. You need to write. This is very good, and I will be telling other people about it." And she did.

You've read this far, so I want you to know that if Mary hadn't encouraged me, I don't know that I would have written this book—or any of the others. When she told me, "You're a good writer ... you need to write," it changed the game for me. It was an ugly duckling moment in my life. So, I wrote, and I keep writing.

But I wonder why I didn't feel like a writer before that. I mean, I'd written quite a bit in my life up to that point. Two novels, half a dozen short stories, articles, and an e-book. Was it that I'd been a good writer before and never had a Mary Kelly to reflect it back to me? Or was it that I developed as a writer and Mary Kelly was there to identify the moment when I became a "good" writer? And does any of that matter? Her affirmation and encouragement did the trick and boosted my confidence enough to fuel millions more words—

who cares how or why it came to be.

What I do know is that there is incredible power in seeing and voicing the potential and possibility in others. I know there are times I've done it by accident, but seeing what it did for me, I want to be more purposeful in affirming what is good in people.

And this brings me to the favor I'd like to ask of you.

One of the most powerful ways we can see and name the good in another person is to say thank you. Specific gratitude that sees the greatness in another person, names it, and explains why it matters is one of the greatest gifts we can give to one another.

In that spirit, would you send a thank you of your own? Send it to someone who needs encouragement, who needs to know your gratitude, or could use a reminder of their greatness. Choose someone you haven't thanked before. Select a person who contributed to your life or the world in a way you know personally.

It is so rare for any of us to know how our actions ripple outward and affect people we'll never know. I'd love for Mary to know that her few words of encouragement for me have rippled outward and benefitted you as well. If it weren't for her words, this book and those that preceded it would never have existed.

If you let me know who you've thanked or encouraged I'll be sure to let Mary know. You can reach me at david.dye@letsgrowleaders.com.

And Mary, if you're reading this: Thank you. Thank you for the generosity of your time, encouragement, and example. For seeing, for saying what you saw, and for fueling my service.

NOT ALONE

"The most terrible poverty is loneliness and the feeling of being unloved."
—Mother Teresa

Do you remember the time in your life when you felt most alone?

For me, it was an evening during a trip to Cambodia. Karin and I had joined some friends and colleagues who work to support non-profits that help women and children throughout Southeast Asia. That evening, ten of us decided to take an ATV tour through parts of rural Cambodia. We set out in groups of four—three of us along with one guide from the company. I was riding the last vehicle in the last group.

Perhaps twenty minutes into our ride, our friend Alex, riding in front of me, overcorrected a turn and flipped her ATV. I watched it roll as if in slow motion, tossing her like a rag doll, until it came to a stop, right side up—on top of her.

I was the only one who saw the accident. The other riders in our group could not hear me honking or shouting over the noise of their engines.

As they receded into the distance, I looked at Alex pinned under her ATV, unsure how badly she was injured. And I felt—alone.

She desperately needed help, but all she had was me. I didn't speak the language, was in the countryside without a clue how to get back to town, and only had a light first-aid kit for scrapes and sprains. I don't think I'll ever forget that sensation: *It's just me.* Followed by, *Well, let's get to it.*

I lifted the ATV off her (the power of adrenaline), began evaluating her injuries, and tried to keep her conscious (a losing effort). Thankfully, there were no compound fractures and her neck and spine seemed to be good, but she had a nasty wound on her chin that was bleeding profusely.

Probably in response to my honking and shouting, several local people came out to see what was happening. I remember one man in particular. He had deeply tanned, leathery skin, and only two teeth remained in his mouth. None of them spoke English, but they conferred among themselves and sent someone off to call for help. By this time, our guide and Karin had looked back and realized Alex and I weren't with them. They retraced their route until they found us.

Alex was losing consciousness and needed to get to a hospital. So, our guide got on his ATV. Karin and the villagers lifted the now-unconscious Alex onto the ATV and seated her directly behind our guide. Then the guide told Karin to get on the ATV behind the two of them.

The man with two teeth wrapped Karin's arms around our friend and made her hold on to the front of the guide, sandwiching Alex between Karin and him. Another local woman clarified what was happening: "You," she pointed at Karin, then waved her hand in the distance, "go hospital."

And with that, the guide took off, driving his ATV cross-country over fields while I was left to watch over my vehicle, Karin's, and the one that had crashed. I gathered up Karin's purse and Alex's cell phone, messaged our group to let them know what had happened, and waited.

Meanwhile, Karin held Alex as they transferred to a tuk-tuk and sped to the hospital. In our discussions afterward, Karin shared how, during that drive to the hospital as she tried to revive and keep our friend conscious, she felt a similar sense of being alone—What should I do? Am I enough in this situation?

She felt alone. I had felt alone.

And yet ...

I wasn't. Not really.

Within moments, there were villagers.

A few moments more, and there was my partner, ready to do what I could not (be the third person on the back of an ATV—no way I would have fit) and then advocate for Alex with the doctors at the hospital.

As I've reflected on that evening, I am touched at the way people came together to help.

In all the craziness that the world throws at us, it's easy to feel alone, but there are so many moments of human kindness and decency every day.

Can we look for them? Contribute to them?

And if you're feeling alone, know that you are enough—do what you can, but please honk the horn and call for help.

Postscript:

Our friend did not escape unscathed: a broken jaw that required surgery, multiple stitches on her chin, and deep gouges to her hands, arms, and elbows. But between her treatment by doctors in Cambodia and then Thailand, she recovered well. Given the severity of the accident, I'm grateful it wasn't worse.

SEEING

"It is a sobering thought that the finest act of love you can perform is not an act of service but an act of contemplation, of seeing. When you serve people, you help, support, comfort, and alleviate pain. When you see them in their inner beauty and goodness, you transform and create."
—Anthony DeMello

I have what my wife calls "adult onset running."

Karin's been an athlete her entire life. A competitive swimmer in her youth, a triathlete in her adult years, and a Boston Marathon qualifier, she's now moved on to road bike races in the Rocky Mountains.

I'm pretty much the opposite. My extracurriculars tended to the debate-tournament end of the spectrum, and my sole running achievement for many years was a ten-minute mile my sophomore year of high school. As an adult, I've enjoyed walking and hiking, and that was always fast enough for me.

But one day in my late thirties, for reasons that are still unclear to me, I decided to run. I was seriously overweight, so running at that point looked more like walking for a hundred paces, jogging for twenty-five paces until I was out of breath, and then repeating it until I had circled the lake in a neighborhood park. Those moments of huffing and puffing led to a 10K, a half-marathon, and now I'm training for my first marathon.

In the process of moving from walker to runner, something interesting happened.

I'd walked these same recreation trails many times before. Oncoming traffic included bikers, runners, three generations of families, and new parents pushing strollers. Occasionally, someone would look up as they passed, make eye contact, and perhaps smile or nod. When I'm walking, it's most often the young parents who greet me as they pass. Never the runners.

Until ...

I change my walk into the slowest of jogging shuffles, and something amazing happens.

The runners see me.

A shirtless man with a Thor-like physique and reflective sunglasses now raises two fingers in a silent semi-salute that says, "Dude, strong work. Look at you out here tearing it up. Clearly you're on your seventeenth mile today since you're shuffling along there. Well done, my man."

At least, that's how I interpret it.

Pick up my pace just a bit, break a sweat, and I go from invisible pedestrian to part of the group. A runner. One of us.

Whether an oncoming runner acknowledges my presence or not won't make or break my day—but it still makes me smile inside.

Years ago, I attended a convention and met a man from Eastern Europe—I cannot place his accent. I'd never met this man before, but as I entered the room, he welcomed me with both arms held out toward me, hands open, a broad smile, and said, "There he is!" He drew out the "there" as if to say, "*Now this* is the person I've been waiting for."

My guess is that he was confused and had mistaken me for someone else. It didn't matter. I involuntarily smiled, and my heart replied, "Well yes, I am here—thanks for noticing!"

These days when I run, I try to acknowledge every person I pass. It doesn't cost much—a tip of the head, a wave, a two-finger Thorsalute. One of the greatest gifts we can give another human being is to see them. Perhaps not when we're racing through crowded sidewalks and subway cars during rush hour—that would be weird. (What does it say about us that seeing the people we pass every day would be weird?)

But life gives us plenty of chances to see one another ... if we only recognize that they are part of our group.

Would anything be more powerful than a chorus of voices from the people we meet, saying, "Yes, I am here—thanks for noticing!"

HOW TO COOK
THANKSGIVING DINNER

"Communication is awful hard between people."
–Tennessee Williams, *Cat on a Hot Tin Roof*

"Is communication even possible?"

I still remember my high school English teacher, Mrs. Roads, asking us that question. We were reading William Faulkner's *The Sound and the Fury*. When your English teacher suggests that real communication is difficult, if not impossible–well, that's a lot to wrap your head around. When I was sixteen, it sounded silly. I mean, sure, we don't always understand each other, but come on! Look around: we communicate all the time and things get done, right? Faulkner's book was an incredible work of art, but his take on the impossibility of ideal communication and human isolation didn't make sense to me.

Not for a while.

"Would you like to cook Thanksgiving dinner with me?"

They were sweet and beautiful words–an invitation from Karin that (to me) signified another level in the earlier years of our relationship. We were dating seriously but still lived in different states. Co-hosting Thanksgiving dinner meant that I would fly to Maryland, Karin would pick up ingredients, and then we'd have a lovely holiday with her family.

That was the plan.

About two hours into our holiday meal preparations, we called a timeout, put our ingredients in the fridge, and went for a walk to talk about what was happening.

It turned out that the words "cook Thanksgiving dinner" meant two significantly different things to each of us. For Karin, they meant a snuggly time in the kitchen, having fun, chopping vegetables, stealing kisses, and stirring pots.

My vision ... was a little more intense.

I love cooking, but the way I prepare large holiday meals—well, let's just say a spreadsheet is often involved. No, not joking. Pair that structured approach with the fact that this was the first time I was cooking for her family (and Karin had regaled her family with tales of my culinary skills), and I was feeling the pressure to deliver.

So, I did what I tend to do in these situations—got super focused on the task and closed out most everything else. In other words, it was not a snuggly time in the kitchen.

Oops.

Thankfully, I have an amazing partner who recognized her own disappointment in what was happening, suggested the timeout, and gave us a chance to talk about our different approaches. We came back stronger and had a great holiday (though my whipped cream never did set). In the years since then, we continue to marvel at how we can hear the same words but when filtered through our own personality and experiences, interpret them so differently. It is a source of rich wonder.

And occasional frustration.

Misunderstandings cause so much pain. What if we truly could understand one another? Would that harm or help? Maybe someday, science will give us a magic "understanding button" that will solve our misunderstandings, but I'm not sure we'd welcome it.

At first you might think such a button would help because we would avoid the problems of misconstrued phrases and words having different meanings. But then you have the problem of actually, honestly knowing what another person is saying without the veil of civil language or cloak of misinterpretation to hide behind. Would that be better, or would there be more hurt feelings with real understanding?

I wonder.

Learning to communicate well is a challenge, but an equally important and practical life skill is learning who a person is and how they use words. Life is easier when you know who you're talking to. If they make a commitment, can you count on it? Are they manipulative and trying to get your buy-in but with no ability, intent, or plan to follow through?

I have a friend who I made plans to meet for a winter hike. We'd made the plans three months earlier, and on the appointed day, a blizzard was raging and the windchill was below zero. I bundled up and went to meet him. He was three minutes late (he'd had to drive fifty miles in driving snow, after all).

We laughed as we met because we'd both considered calling to confirm that we were still on for our hike. But then we thought about who we were meeting—if they said they'd be there, they'd be there, no matter if it was three months ago and the weather today was freezing.

I had another friend who always said he'd be there.

Birthday party on Saturday? "I'll see you there."

Reunion of friends for beer and cards? "Definitely—that will be awesome."

Chance that he'd actually show up? Around one in four. And no, he didn't call to say he wouldn't be there. The rest of us learned to enjoy his company when he was there but never to count on him—that would guarantee disappointment 75 percent of the time.

I worked with a guy once who needed a formula filter. You had to divide any number he gave you in half. So, if he said, "This is easily a thousand people," you'd know that it was five hundred people, maybe.

So maybe Mrs. Roads and Faulkner had a point.

Can we communicate perfectly with one another?

No.

But the next question is more important: How can we be on a journey of learning to be understood and to understand others?

Maybe communication is imperfect, but it sure beats the alternatives.

INTERLUDE II

CANDLE PARTY

"Do not worry if all the candles in the world flicker and die.
We have the spark that starts the fire."
–Rumi

My daughter's friend has a side business facilitating make-your-own-candle parties. That's remarkable. Candles have been around for at least five thousand years, and we can still have parties devoted to them.

I wonder what the first candle-users would make of our relationship with candles? Would the ancient Egyptians and Chinese marvel at our use of wick and wax for recreation? Or would they nod knowingly when we light the wicks to sanctify or celebrate? Would they participate in a candle-making party and share a few of their own carefully guarded techniques?

It's been less than one hundred years since we outgrew our dependence on candles for light. We've needed candles for pragmatic, functional light for 98.2 percent of the time we've had them. Will we ever outgrow our love of wax and flame? Or are candles such a deeply ingrained part of human life that they'll be with us for centuries to come?

I confess: I love candles. Something is magical about that little flame.

Sometimes, when I face endless days at my desk, I will light a candle to signal the beginning of work or writing and blow it out when a chapter is complete. Karin and I celebrated our wedding with a candle. We light it every year on our anniversary. We light candles to accompany our evening meals. We light several in carved pumpkins every October to entertain, if not scare away the fey and evil spirits.

My sister loves the uniquely scented candles from her favorite home-goods store and stocks up when sales and coupons align to get her through the winter with cozy warm aromas and flickering light. I remember attending a Pioneer Days as a child, where I learned to make a candle by repeatedly dipping a wick in melted wax (I'm assuming the make-your-own-candle parties are more fun).

We light candles to start a moment or signal a sacred time. To warm a room, to scent a space, to set a mood. We light candles for romance, to remember, to commemorate. In the darkest winter days, we light candles and pass the flame to celebrate the return of light and hope.

It's a funny relationship we have with these delightful little flames. A functional tool we relied on for millennia is now a focus of parties, romance, and commemoration. I wonder what tools we depend on today that will someday be decorative and a theme for parties?

It's a funny relationship we have with candles but one I hope we never lose.

SECTION III

EMBERS AND
HIDDEN TREASURES

"There are stores that enrich the streets with their presence, and the most precious of them are the shops that sells old books!"
—Mehmet Murat ildan

I love the anticipation of entering a used bookstore. There is always a chance that, tucked away in a back corner between last year's rejected pop-psychology and ragged well-loved summer thrillers, you can find a treasure. Perhaps it's a classic that escaped your attention earlier in life. Maybe it's a bit of wisdom or enlightenment. It's a rare and elusive treasure to find, and yet, hope and the hunt go on because you never know what you'll discover.

One childhood summer, I was in the car with a friend and his mom on the way to a hike, and his mom stopped at a small-town mountain antique store. The curios and antiques spilled out of racks and shelves in the converted gas station's service bay. I came across a coat of arms and two crossed swords. It was forty-five dollars—a fortune for me at that age that I could never afford. Which was for the best because it was the joyous kind of discovery that would have been an albatross once I got it home and searched my room for the wall space to display it.

The Pike Place Market in Seattle, Camden Lock Market in London, the sprawling Chatuchak Market in Bangkok, and every farmers market I've ever visited are labyrinths of discoveries waiting to be made. Level upon level ... just around every corner is the possibility

of finding—what exactly? A treasure? A truly magical device or word or idea? Peace? The secret to that unknown world that hovers, waiting, just beyond ours—if only you have the right key? It is the delight of movies like *ET*, *Gremlins*, *Goonies*, and *Harry Potter*. That encounter with mystery, the beyond; the thrill of discovery, of adventure.

But adult-me wonders. Are there any more undiscovered curiosities? Or are there only piles of junk, discards, and manufactured trinkets with their false promises of contentment? Castoff things without a home. And if there were a secret world and place to be discovered and explored ... how long until it, too, was known, exploited, and filled with dross?

Despite my grown-up cynicism, the hunt continues. I cannot approach bookstores and markets without a thrill and secret hope that this time ... this time I will find that curiosity. That key. That wonder.

And sometimes, I do.

Perhaps the real adventures are the ones we give ourselves. The adventures of growing, building, loving, and exploring the wide real world and galaxy beyond.

There are no portals to secret worlds, no wands to make a car fly, but ... a story shared, a perspective that enlightens and calms, and words that bring peace or stir to action. Every bit as wonderful and transformative and real, these curios, mysteries, and memories do exist. These are the magical embers and coals ... waiting, biding their time to be discovered, brushed off, and brought to life. Henri Nouwen wrote, "One of the most satisfying aspects of writing is that it can open in us deep wells of hidden treasures that are beautiful for us as well as for others to see." I have found it to be so.

These embers, coals, and hidden treasures often do their best work in moments of silence or sadness. This section features those moments.

We begin with silence.

THE QUIET

"There is a beginning. There is no beginning of that beginning.
There is something. There is nothing."
—Chuang Tzu

A moment of calm occurs just before water boils.

The pot shakes and makes a racket as the water vibrates with energy. The noise builds to a crescendo, and then, a moment before the water begins to boil, there is a pause, a quiet, as if the water has done its work and is gathering itself for the boiling ahead.

There is a similar pause and quiet in the fireplace when the flames die down and the coals burn red. You put a fresh log on the coals and gently blow. The first breath stirs some ash, and the coals burn more brightly. The second breath brings the coals to full orange attention. Then, with the third breath, nothing seems to happen—for a moment. There is a pause, and then a new flame appears. Sometimes a whole rush of them, as the fire is reinvigorated by the oxygen you've fed it.

In that pause before the water boils or the flames ignite, it can feel like nothing's happening.

But it is.

Can you trust the pause and embrace the quiet that portends the boil and the flame?

SILENT CRAFT

"Quiet is peace."
-Khaled Hosseini, *The Kite Runner*

Every Friday morning, the most popular morning radio show in town hosted Live Audience Friday. A group of twelve people were allowed into the broadcast booth to watch the three show hosts do their thing.

I'd listened to their show for years. Every morning, they reliably bantered for four hours, making me smile, laugh, reflect, and, a time or two, even cry. Between songs and commercials, they played games, shared trivia, commented on the events of the day, held contests, and shared observations they'd made about life and the oddities of human behavior.

The three of them had incredible chemistry. They were a joy. Over the years as I drove my daughter to school and then drove myself to work, they felt like friends. And, after years of listening to Live Audience Friday, my sister, her husband, and I decided it was our turn to visit and experience the magic.

When our morning arrived, we met outside in the chilly morning dark while most of the world slept, filed into the studio, and waited for the magic to happen.

The show was as enjoyable as I hoped; the hosts' interactions with the audience were kind, fun, and uplifting. But what struck me most about watching these three create their on-air repartee ... was the silence.

When the on-air sign lit up, they were full of life, connected to one another, and poured energy across the airwaves into their hundreds of thousands of listeners. But when the sign went dark, they went silent. They studied notes, occasionally asked a quiet question of one another, and generally said very little.

It was the opposite of what I'd expected. My impression as a listener was that what we heard on our radios was the on-air continuation of an ongoing conversation that we'd been allowed to listen in on.

In hindsight, that sense of connection and ongoing conversation was the result of the hosts' craft and professionalism. They were good at what they did—and that included those moments of silence when they gathered their energy, reviewed the content they had prepared, and did the work to deliver a best-in-class show.

During the COVID-19 pandemic, Karin and I moved our entire business to live-remote delivery. Some days featured five or six hours on-camera, engaging leaders around the world in human-centered leadership practices and skills. Over the many months of pandemic-enforced remote programs, I've often thought of those radio hosts' silent moments.

When we turn off the camera for a breakout session, group discussion, or pause between programs, Karin and I study our notes, return emails, and exchange a quiet question or two.

In the silence of craft and professionalism.

THAT'S SAD

"He wanted to know before he learned, but learning takes time."
—John Morelock, *Run Gently Out There*

It's a critical life skill they don't teach you in school. Like doing your taxes, buying a car, or plugging in a USB drive correctly on the first try. (And if you're reading this in the future and don't know what a USB drive is, well, then the future turned out well in at least one respect—be grateful!)

The untaught lesson is the skill of feeling sad. Though my son points out that while you may not learn *how* to be sad in school, you do get lots of practice.

Many people never learn how to be sad, or they spend years trying to avoid sadness altogether. Culturally speaking, people in the United States don't do sad. Happy, entertained, and distracted are feelings we do well. We're good at anger and indignation. But sadness—that's just a bummer, and who needs that in their life?

I do, for one.

And I'm pretty sure you do, too.

I've had plenty to feel sad about. I grew up in pretty messed-up circumstances. My parents belonged to a religious semi-cult. We weren't secluded in a compound or anything; I attended elementary school like any other child. But unlike the other children, my parents were unduly influenced by the leader of the church who cultivated dependence on him to interpret God's will, who took sexual liberties with women, and who convinced members to take jobs that were substantially beneath their ability and education. These unskilled jobs prevented members from realizing their agency in life and kept them dependent on the leader. As a child, I learned that every head cold I had was an indication that I was "out of God's will"—in sin somewhere in my life. You can imagine what that does to a kid.

My Saturday nights were a mix of joy and dread. Joy because *The Muppet Show* aired on Saturday nights, and I loved it. That Henson humor. Beautiful interpretations of music. Wondrous set pieces with singing flowers and trees. And the inevitable sketches that ended with explosions or penguins being tossed in the air (or maybe it was chickens). I loved the Muppets.

But several decades later, I still remember the dread that grew in my gut and undercut the show's fun. I remember complaining to my parents of feeling unwell, of stomachaches. I wasn't sick. At least not physically. I just didn't want to go to Sunday school the next morning. And not because it was boring. I liked the other kids, and we could have fun together in other settings.

It was our teacher.

Her tools of discipline and order were screaming and derision. Color outside a line, and she mocked you and compared you to other children who'd managed to do it right. And if you had the bad luck to break something, not through abuse or intention but just the normal collateral damage of kids being kids, oh, it was bad. She would tear you down, screaming, spit flying, flaying your dignity as the other kids silently grieved for you while also giving thanks that they'd escaped this time.

There was an erasable whiteboard on the basement wall, and one time I used one of the markers to make a small mark in the corner. Just experimenting with the wonder of erasable markers. It was a marvel! (This was a sure sign I was destined to be a teacher, consultant, and trainer. Who likes whiteboards more?)

But when she saw the unsanctioned line ... half an inch of unapproved green ink marring her perfect board ... she lost it. She screamed at all of us, demanding to know who had done such a thing. I fessed up. Staying silent only prolonged the tirade, and after all, hadn't we learned that Jesus sacrificed himself to save everyone else? And he wasn't even guilty like I was.

I'd made the mark, after all. I endured the screams and criticisms. Years later when I read *Harry Potter* and met Dolores Umbridge, I recognized her. If my Sunday school teacher would have had Umbridge's pen that carved lines into my hand, she would have used it.

I know now that it was emotional abuse. I know today that she suffered some kind of mental illness—she wasn't well, and children should never have been left in her care. I can interpret all that happened through those nice explainy words. But I am sad for that child ... for all of the children who suffered that torment. It wasn't right. It was wrong. I hurt for those children. And I'm sad that the weekly anticipation of her abuse poisoned my joyful Muppets.

By middle school, my parents divorced. My four youngest siblings lived with my mom, while my oldest sister and I lived with my father. (These were voluntary choices but also a function of the space available in each household.) As I mentioned in the introduction, during my freshman year of college, my father told us he was gay and was leaving to live with his new partner.

I'd been planning on living at home that summer and scrambled to find a place to live. My mom's house was overflowingly full, so I got a two-bedroom apartment and invited my sister to live with me while she finished high school. My apartment was an hour and a half bus ride from campus, so between work, classes, and bus commutes, I didn't have a typical college experience.

Back then, there was no time to feel sad, nor did I know how. Feeling sad for the loss of my childhood, of my parents, of the college experience others might have, wasn't an option. I couldn't put my feelings into words back then, but my fear was that if I let myself feel sad for anything, it would overwhelm me. Paralyze me. That would be the end of everything. So I smiled and got on with living as best I could.

That started to change shortly after I finished college, when I got a phone call. The phone call was about a man named Mick.

When I was a child, Mick was our most frequent babysitter. He was a gentle but firm surrogate parent with ample love to give. He lived alone with three miniature dogs and a cat. He volunteered as a chaplain at a local youth detention facility and also spent hours each week picking up donated bread and produce to distribute to people in need. When I was a car-less teenager, he lent me his car many times to help me with work or fun (and I know I'm not the only one).

Mick had had polio as a child, and his arms didn't work properly. One of them was withered, and he couldn't do much with it—he would sort of throw this shoulder forward or back, and the momentum would carry that arm where he wanted it to go. His other arm worked well enough for him to drive and get through life.

The October after I graduated from college, I got a phone call.

Mick had been murdered.

Two of the kids (fourteen and sixteen years old) that he'd chaplained at the detention facility had been released. They hadn't seen Mick as a caring, life-changing soul. They saw him as an easy mark who couldn't defend himself. As near as we could tell from their statements to police and the physical evidence, when they showed up, Mick invited them in. When he understood that they meant to rob him, he told them to take it all with his blessing. Very Bishop Myriel in *Les Misérables*, yes. That was Mick. They killed him anyway with a large knife.

It was the first time I encountered the full stages of grief. The denial and bargaining as your brain refuses to accept what has happened. The rage. I went to a park and tried to pull a rotten tree out of the ground and throw it. And eventually, the depression, anger again, and sadness came in seemingly endless waves.

This I could be sad about—how could you not? And for the first time in my life, I let the sadness and grief do their work. I didn't realize it at the time, but I'd learned something: the sadness wouldn't end me.

Feeling sad is a life skill.

It may feel scary, but it's worth the risk. I've had plenty to feel sad about … and I know you have, too. In my adult life, that's included professional betrayals, the end of a marriage, and a suicide attempt by a close family member. Yours will be different, but they are there, and they are real.

Allow the pain to flow. Acknowledge the loss and experience the peace that comes after a storm has passed.

EMOTIONAL ECOLOGY

"What would an ocean be without a monster lurking in the dark?"
—Werner Herzog

As someone who grew up thousands of miles from the nearest ocean, I always found huge bodies of water to be mysterious and slightly menacing. What will you find in the depths? I would look at the surface of the ocean and wonder. How deep? How toothy? How sharp, poisonous, or slimy is what lurks beneath the surface?

Then I got my first chance to snorkel. I put on fins and goggles that magically revealed the vibrant (and yes, sometimes pointy and poisonous) world beneath the waves. The variety of colors and creatures was breathtaking. In the years that followed, I would never forget the hidden world just beneath the gray-blue surface, but the ocean was still mysterious, still menacing.

Then I discovered scuba. With a tank of air, I was no longer floating above that magical world, looking at it as a tourist. For the forty-five or fifty minutes the air lasts, scuba lets you become part of the reef. You swim with the fish, alongside the ray, nose-to-nose with the sea lion.

There are still vast stretches of open water ... looking "into the blue" (away from the reef—out into the open water) is awe-inspiring and overwhelming, like looking into the night sky and seeing how small you are in comparison. And sometimes you're rewarded with a view of a bigger creature swimming farther out from the reef where they have more room.

The world beneath the waves frightened me until I was able to explore it. Seeing the depths in detail made them more familiar. But those first moments of exploration aren't easy—submerging, wondering what you'll find and if you can trust your air, and overcoming your body's urge to say, "I shouldn't be here."

There is angst in looking deep inside, as well. What will I see as I confront my own subconscious? What ugliness and undesirable traits swim beneath the surface? Will some dark impulse consume me in rending toothy bites if I dip my head in that water? Will I drown in the weight of sadness if I let myself experience it?

Some people embrace the leviathan lurking in the depths. They revel in their rage and jealousy, give them full expression ... and usually aren't fun to be around. But not me; my dysfunction went the other way: bury, suppress, and deny. Perhaps if I didn't acknowledge its existence, the ugliness I found—the resentments, envy, frustrations, lust, and grief—these all-too-human emotions, would go away.

But to ignore the emotions swimming below the surface either makes them stronger or divides your soul from itself. Diving beneath the ocean waves and exploring the beauty, wonder, and danger is like acknowledging and exploring those emotions. To see them, watch them swim, and understand their ecology allows you to understand what you're feeling and why you're feeling it. Gives you a chance to acknowledge it, let it swim on, or do something about it. Respond to it. Learn from it.

Sometimes those scary, ugly emotions tell you something important. They are a warning or alert to do something differently. Giving voice to my anger, I learn what it has to tell me. Does it protect me against injustice or alert me that my ego was bruised, and there is room for me to learn more deeply and release pride? Or both?

Dive in and swim around with your sadness, your anger, your envy.

Let them swim by and see how they live and what they're for. As you experience them, they loosen their grip. They don't shout for attention so loudly, and rather than take over and consume you (which was often my fear), they do their work and swim on.

HEADSHOTS

"You have to be a bit of a liar to tell a story the right way.
Too much truth confuses the facts. Too much honesty
makes you sound insincere."
—Patrick Rothfuss, *The Name of the Wind*

When your work puts you in the public eye, it's common to have a professional headshot—a photograph for the back of books, conference signage, and a million internet profiles. You can look mine up easily: do a quick image search for "David Dye author." (That will filter out the David Dye NPR radio host. If you see a beard, that's him, not me.)

My headshot was taken by AJ, a very talented photographer who likes for her photographs to tell a story. And this one does. It's the story of a guy who is confident and clever. An Author and International Speaker (spoken in a deep, resonant voice), smiling at an inside joke that must have been good. He's accomplished and successful, the guy in that photo. I love that picture.

And I loathe it.

The photo tells a story, but it doesn't tell the whole story. It's easy to look at that photo and for me to see JAWG (just another white guy).

The photograph doesn't tell the story of the kid who suffered emotional abuse from those who should help and protect. The years growing up in a toxic religion. The kid whose parents screamed until they left. The boy who loved to walk to a local stream by himself and spend the day catching crawdads and splashing through cool water.

The picture doesn't tell the story of poverty, government cheese, and the playground shame of ragged jeans whose patches had patches, of friends moving away as their parents found better jobs or were promoted. Of finding a loved one in the basement barely breathing with a plastic bag around her head, a victim of her inner demons. It doesn't tell the story of a kid in college with nowhere to call home. Of caring for his sister while she finished high school. Of years spent teaching and mentoring children who received poor starting cards at life's poker table. Does it tell the story of friends and siblings who show up, no matter what? Of all the breaking and growing that is life?

The photo tells a story—but is it the whole story?

Maybe the picture does tell these stories, in its own way. The story of someone who cares because he knows what it is to hurt. The story of someone who can smile because he viscerally values love, laughter, and friendship.

As I think about the picture that represents me to the world, I challenge myself: Can I look behind the photos of others to see the whole person? To see their joy, their pain, their triumphs, and their suffering? In a world where so many of the pictures we share are carefully curated to tell a story of an impossible life, what would it look like to tell the full story? The one we can all relate to because we live it, too?

INTERLUDE III

UNBIDDEN WORDS

"Language is a city to the building of which
every human being brought a stone."
–Ralph Waldo Emerson

A word came to mind this morning, unbidden.

It was the right word, though one I have never written nor spoken aloud. I was just writing along, minding my own business, when *ta-da!* There it was, ready to be added to the page.

That's strange, I thought. I've never used that word before. Can it really mean what I think it means?

So, I looked up the definition and, sure enough, it was the correct word.

How does this happen?

I've experienced this a couple of times: a word suddenly popping into my head, feeling both new and right. Logically, I know I must have read these words somewhere and picked up their meaning from context, but I couldn't tell you where. And that feels magical. My multilingual friends tell me this is a common experience for them. They need the word in one language and magically discover it coming to mind in another language.

Is there a word for this experience when the right word comes to mind when you've never written or spoken that word before?

If not, perhaps we can Shakespeare a new word to describe it.

I will propose "sermoccurrence."

Please send me your nominations: david.dye@letsgrowleaders.com.

Is this phenomenon a corrective force?

Perhaps the universe restores the balance for those more common times when a word is on the tip of your tongue and you can't quite recall it when you need it. There is a word for this; it's called lethologica. How odd that we have a word for when you can't remember a word but not for the opposite.

My friend James pointed out that it would be cruel to mention a word coming to mind and never mention what that word was. The word was liminal—which I used in that moment to describe the transition between night and day.

What a great word. I leave you now in the liminal space between this interlude and the next section.

SECTION IV

FOLLOW THE MUSIC

"Willing is doing something you know already, something you have been told by somebody else; there is no new imaginative understanding in it. And presently your soul gets frightfully sterile and dry because you are so quick, snappy, and efficient about doing one thing after another that you have not time for your own ideas to come in and develop and gently shine."
–Brenda Ueland, *If You Want to Write*

I am a planner. That's probably not a surprise after you learned my approach to cooking Thanksgiving dinner, right?

Not always, not perfectly, but in general, I tend to be thinking ahead and organizing my future. What's for dinner, what run I'll do in three weeks, what mountain I'll hike up in two months. One time my daughter stopped me as I walked through the kitchen and asked me why I was carrying some tools, mail, and a throw pillow. I explained that I was going to return the tools to the neighbor, but that on the way, I would leave the pillow in the living room, drop off the mail, and, once the tools were delivered, on the way back inside, I would grab a package from the porch. She shook her head (probably sorry she'd asked) and said, "Do you have to plan every minute?"

So yeah, I'm wired that way.

Which is why this particular hallway conversation was memorable.

Her words came in an offhand comment. Something she probably forgot she said. Three words that made me pause and linger over them. And they opened my life in ways fun and profound.

I was attending a three-day conference in Washington, D.C. The final evening's dinner and awards ceremony had concluded, and I was walking down a hallway, trying to decide what to do next. My flight home would leave the next morning, which meant I had several hours available to do ... what? I wasn't sure.

That's when my friend walked by, going the other direction.

"Hey David, what are you up to?" she asked.

I shrugged. "At the moment, I'm a planner without a plan."

She smiled and said, "Follow the music!" and walked off down the hall.

Follow the music. Hmm. I'm sure I looked silly standing in the hallway looking up and to the side, contemplating the words. Those three little words may not sound like much, but they were a big deal.

I'd read enough fairy tales, Tolkien, and Homer to know what can happen when you follow the music. Get captured by wood elves and thrown into a Mirkwood dungeon, or shipwrecked and drowned by sirens–that's what. You follow the music deeper and deeper into a dark forest until you're lost and ensnared by a trickster whose life and perspective are so far different than humans that you're a plaything in their capricious games. Puck and Nick Bottom would entertain for a moment, but then you wake up with the head of a jackass.

Despite all these literary warnings (which I'm sure were valuable when fairies roamed the earth), I pondered the advice, and a little key turned somewhere in my mind and opened a door. A door that allowed not-knowing, a renewed call to adventure, exploration, and discovery. The words tumbled around my head, refusing to say their piece and move on.

So, follow the music I did. Literally.

I listened and–there was music playing! (Yes, I know it was a metaphor, but you must start somewhere.) That night, I followed the music, found the dance floor, and spent those hours dancing in what turned out to be my second-all-time-favorite non-wedding dance party.

A few days later, I was speaking at a conference in Portland, Oregon, and once again took the advice literally. This time, I followed the music to a downtown street corner where a two-man didgeridoo band played multiple didgeridoos along with other percussion and techno. Weird and fun. Another time when we were working in Dublin, Ireland, following the music led to a street performer playing a beautiful rendition of the Game of Thrones theme on his guitar.

So yeah, I literally followed the music (and still do—I love the generosity and beauty of random live music and always tip if I have cash on me).

But of course, the words were a metaphor. What of the music of life?

For me, the music is the call of the words I need to write. The work I need to do. The song of the mountains that summons me to hours of solitude and camaraderie on the trail.

Following the music led me to my partnership with Karin, our family, the business we've built, the books we've written, and the many amazing people we've worked with. Following the music has taken me to the most extraordinary places. A seawall in California where a wave leapt up and drenched us. The Giant's Causeway in Ireland. Stumbling upon a Banksy mural in Bristol, England. Singing at the top of our lungs in a piano bar in Austin, Texas (literal again, I know), sharing a midnight fire with a bachelor party and delivering an impromptu leadership training session (they asked, I swear), and building clean-water wells in Cambodia and meeting the families who so need the water.

I'm still a planner. But I've gotten more comfortable with not having a plan, seeing what happens, and creating space for serendipity. As Ira Glass, the host of This American Life, says, "If you want lightning to strike, you have to wander around in the rain a lot." In this

94

section, we'll follow the music to look at different (and contradictory) strategies for success in life.

Where will your music lead you?

RADIO PROVIDENCE

"The gods give to mortals not everything at the same time."
—Homer

Do you prefer your music from playlists or providence?

Let me explain ...

I didn't attend my local high school. At the end of eighth grade, one of our teachers recommended five of us to an academically advanced program at a high school across town. I signed up and, along with three of my best friends, started ninth grade at George Washington High School.

It didn't take long before I became aware that things were different. My friends and I came from working-class households or poverty. Not so for many of my new classmates. They skied in the winter, their families took trips abroad in the summer, and their clothes spoke of a different economy. The schoolwork was different as well. I'd been a straight-A student and had never found school very challenging. Until now. It took real effort to keep up.

The new people, harder work, and my adolescent insecurity mixed together to form a potent cocktail of self-doubt. I'm sure they would cringe to hear it now, but my fourteen-year-old self was certain the teachers thought I didn't belong there and were doing what they could to pile on the work and force me to bow out of the program.

It's ridiculous, I know, but I'd concocted this story, and heading into the holidays of my first year, I doubted whether I would make it. Mendelian genetics was there to put the nail in the coffin. The crucible of freshman biology was a massive genetics problem where peas had been crossed, different color flowers bloomed, and your task was to discern what the invisible DNA and genes were doing behind the scenes. Mr. Counts always assigned this project over the winter intermission—because that's the way Brother Mendel intended it? Other teachers, knowing the days of work these peas would consume, mercifully kept their assignments light.

After five hours wrestling with those peas at the kitchen table, my insecurity peaked. I was done. The peas were too much. The program was too much. It was time to throw in the towel. I'd get through Christmas and the New Year, go back to school, and transfer out at the semester break.

I set my pencil on the table and stared at the sheets of notebook paper covered with letters, arrows, and erased smudges, contemplating my decision. Regret and relief battled for supremacy.

That's when I became aware of the radio. I often work to music and had turned on the radio when I sat down to focus on the project. The music had been background noise until then. The Little River Band started singing about a Lonesome Loser, a song I'd heard many times before. But this time, the first verse grabbed my attention. It was about a loser who keeps on trying but is still a loser.

If the opening lines made me pay attention, the second verse was a bucket of cold water in my face. The lyrics challenge you to sit down and take a look at yourself. To face the reality that you can't run from yourself.

It was like they'd written those first two stanzas just for me, an insecure fourteen-year-old kid who felt sorry for himself because he didn't fit in. Because, for the first time in his life, school wasn't easy.

I responded immediately. "No! I don't want to be a lonesome loser. I do want to be somebody. I have to face this? Fine. I won't run and hide."

Perhaps the Queen of Hearts was a stand-in for the peas, or freshman biology, or the teachers, or all of it. Regardless, she wouldn't beat me. Not this time. I sat up straight. I stopped feeling sorry for myself, picked up the pencil, and figured out the damn peas.

For the rest of high school, I never looked back; that was the last time I thought about quitting. (In fact, I became friends with several of those same teachers I'd miscast as "out to get me.") In a few minutes, that one song, written ten years earlier and performed by an Australian band, came through the radio to change my life.

My friend Matthew and I were discussing this moment in my life and how the right song at the right time can make all the difference. We call it *radio providence* (and I'm pretty sure he deserves full credit for the name).

Radio providence is different than the choice you make to play a song you know suits your mood. It's not an exercise playlist. The universe brings you that song at that moment—and it's perfect. It's providence precisely because it's unexpected and you didn't ask for it.

Most of the time, radio providence isn't life-changing like it was for me that winter day at my kitchen table. It's Sara Bareilles's "Brave" encouraging you to speak your truth when you need to confront a colleague's broken commitment. Or Dee Snyder helping you realize that you're not gonna take it anymore. That your breakup isn't forever, and while it hurts, you'll love again. That tonight actually is going to be a good night.

Encouragement, solace, courage, and joy. Radio providence brings all these and more. When I'm asked by younger people why I don't listen to the cultivated playlists offered on many music platforms, I answer, "Radio providence." There's no fulfillment if I've picked everything.

The perseverance I found in those allele-filled days before Christmas has served me many times in life. I sometimes wonder how my life would have turned out had that song not played at that moment. Would I have found resiliency and determination another way? Would I have left that school, the friends I made, and the path my education set me down?

There's no way to know. What I do know is that today, I have a playlist for my workouts, but I still hit "shuffle." As any student of Greek mythology will tell you, it's better not to mess with Fate.

GAS STATION

"Open your eyes and see what you can with them before they close forever."
—Anthony Doerr, *All the Light We Cannot See*

Have you ever been upset with someone for telling you what you really needed to hear? Yeah, me too.

If you've been to a gas station in a rougher part of town, then you're familiar with what we called "the cage." Floor-to-ceiling bulletproof glass surrounding the cashier on every side to keep them safe. I worked at one of these gas stations between my senior year of high school and my freshman year of college.

On a steamy night in July, I started my first week of graveyard shifts and was trained in how to operate the cage. There were two critical pieces of equipment. One was a deadbolt lock on the bulletproof glass door leading in and out. The other was a toggle switch anchored underneath the cash register. This toggle switch locked and unlocked the outside door—to allow customers in or to lock them out when you would go out to clean or stock the shelves.

During Monday night on my first solo graveyard shift, I was a diligent switch-flipper. I entered the cage, locked the deadbolt, flipped the switch, allowed customers in. When it was time to clean, I flipped the switch, unlocked the deadbolt, stepped out of the cage, and cleaned until a customer knocked or rattled the doors, asking to be let in. Then I stepped back into the cage, locked the deadbolt, flipped the switch, and allowed customers in.

Tuesday night—well, I was young, and flipping the switch seemed like a lot of unnecessary work.

At 1:00 a.m., it was time to wrap hot dog buns. I didn't lock the front door. I left the cage, stationed myself just two feet from the safety of the cage door and with a clear line of sight to the front door to see any customers that might come in, and I started wrapping hot dog buns to be placed in the steamer.

Midway through my third bun, a man's scream interrupted me.

"What are you doing!!??"

I hadn't seen anyone come in ... but standing in front of me was this man with a bushy white beard stained yellow with nicotine. And his coveralls ... they were gray, threadbare, and stained with coffee, grease, and ... is that mustard?

His breath was foul as he put his finger in my chest and shouted in my face, "Don't you ever leave that glass!"

He waved his hand to indicate the whole building. "My brother was shot and killed in a gas station just like this one. Don't you ever leave that glass!" Then he turned on his heel, stomped out the door, got into a beat-up work truck, and drove away.

Do you remember when you were eighteen?

Teenagers aren't always the smartest, and I was no exception.

I fumed.

How dare he? Who does that mustard-stained old man think he is, sneaking in here, getting in my face, and yelling at me? Look, I'm sorry about his brother, but that does not give him the right to scare me like that!

But I *was* scared.

And so, at 3:00 a.m. when it was time to wipe down the counter-tops, I waited for all the customers to leave, and I flipped the toggle switch to lock the front door. I worked my way around the lobby, cleaning counters, until I heard a customer rattle the doors, trying to get in.

So I went back into the cage, locked the door's deadbolt, and flipped the toggle to let the customer come in.

But no one entered the store. I assumed they'd lost patience and left, so I locked up and went back to my cleaning.

Until three police cars pulled into the lot. The three squad cars flipped on their spotlights: all targeted at a dumpster enclosure just to the north of our building.

You see, they were chasing a man who had just committed armed robbery a few blocks down the road. A man who, in his flight from the police, had come upon a brightly lit, twenty-four-hour gas station with a teenage kid whose back was turned to the doors.

Doors that, until a few hours before ... had been unlocked.

The next morning as I pedaled my bike home, I trembled. I began realizing what my arrogance could have cost me.

I'd judged the way he looked, and he didn't talk to me the way I thought I deserved, but that mustard-stained man might have saved my life. At the very least, he kept me from being held hostage.

As time went by and I could reflect on that Tuesday night in July, I resolved that I would never again miss a message because of the mustard.

Life puts all sorts of people in your path. People who will share wisdom, enrich your life - or maybe even keep you from being held hostage by an armed robber. But you have to pay attention, stay humble, and look for it. Because sometimes that wisdom isn't friendly ... it's stained with mustard, wears faded overalls, and screams with pain and anger.

GETTING SMALL

"I cannot do
All the good
That the world needs
But the world
Needs all the good
That I can do."
–Jana Stanfield

What weighs, on average, just over a hundred million tons?

Hint: it floats.

Another hint: it can fuel a daydream, cause joy, or bring death, destruction, and despair.

In 1845, you could not find a single suspension bridge used for trains anywhere in the world. In fact, US engineers dismissed suspension bridges as unsafe in general, much less for a railroad. By 1855, however, the world's first functional railway suspension bridge had been built–spanning the Niagara River and allowing train travel between the United States and Canada.

The bridge started with a picnic and a letter. A Canadian entrepreneur named William Merritt was enjoying a picnic with his wife on the

103

banks of the Niagara River. They'd received a letter from their children, who were visiting Europe. In the letter, the children described an amazing suspension bridge they'd seen in Switzerland. The letter sparked a vision in Merritt to see a similar bridge across the Niagara River, but one capable of rail travel, to connect Canadian trade with the rapidly expanding US rail network and the American West. So he did what visionary entrepreneurs do—got permission from the government, formed a company, and looked for someone with the technical know-how to make it happen.

That someone was an engineer named Charles Ellet, Jr. In addition to his engineering skills, Ellet had a flair for the dramatic. His ability for self-promotion helped him win the contract, and in 1848, he got started, in typical Ellet fashion, with a contest.

Ellet and his team's first problem was how to suspend a line across the gap. It was the narrowest point of the gorge but still 800 feet across and 230 feet deep. The team considered tying a line to cannonballs or a rocket and firing them across the gorge, but they settled on a different strategy. A strategy Leonardo da Vinci suggested four hundred years earlier: use a kite.

For Ellet, this was an opportunity to promote the project (and, I imagine, to prevent newspaper stories of grown men flying kites while they're supposed to be building a bridge). He publicized the event and held a competition with a prize of $5.00 to the boy who first flew a kite across the Niagara Gorge. Many boys from towns on the US side of the river tried and failed. But one boy, Homan Walsh, took a ferry across the river to the Canadian side of the gorge, returned downriver to the gorge, and flew his kite from there. He succeeded on his second attempt and tied his kite string to a tree.

Ellet tied a thicker string to the kite string and pulled it across the gorge. He and his team repeated that operation, tying thicker ropes, pulling them across the gorge, until finally they could pull a cable across. The bridge was underway. (It would require seven more years and a different engineer to finish the job.)

I often think about that bridge. Strong enough to carry loaded trains, but it started with a picnic, a letter, and a kite string. Whenever I'm starting a project that feels overwhelming, I look for the kite string. What's the smallest activity I can do to get started? Towers will need to be built and thick cables secured, but it starts with that string.

Small is powerful.

A kite string is almost beneath notice, but the rail bridge was the first of its kind. A snowflake is inconsequential but an avalanche unstoppable. Back to our opening question: What weighs more than a hundred tons, floats, and causes both daydreams and ruin? The answer is a cloud. (Despite their weight, they are slightly less dense than the surrounding air and so a hundred-ton cloud can hang in the air.)

Vincent van Gogh said, "Great things are not done by impulse, but by a series of small things brought together." He probably wasn't thinking about clouds, avalanches, or rail bridges, but the principle holds true. The power of small—a small habit, repeated daily—will transform your life. A small act of defiance against injustice, replicated across a people, can change a nation. A little bit saved every day becomes a fortune over time.

But it can be hard to show up every day and write, or run, or eat well, or be kind, or stand up for what's right. There are days I don't feel like doing any of those things. And the challenge is, of course, what does one day matter? What if I don't run today? What if I don't write?

And one day may not be a problem ... resting may even be a benefit if I recharge. Refresh; clear the cache. But it is also easy for one day skipped to turn into two. And soon, a habit of absence exists, and the habit of activity must be rebuilt. It's easier to take a step if you've taken a step before. Inertia matters.

Of course, we struggle to see the effect of one run. One ten-minute writing exercise. One word spoken in kindness, a phone call made to a friend or loved one, or another voice raised. The effect of that one moment or action in isolation might not be much at all.

But that small action is not isolated.

You cannot pull the middle thread out of a towel without ruining the whole. So it is with relationships, health, and many areas of life. A series of small, incremental moments that connect and build one upon another to create greatness.

Where can you get small?

VIOLENT THE DAY

"Conquerors live in dread of the day when they are shown to be,
not superior, but simply lucky."
—N.K. Jemisin, *The Stone Sky*

I started the day as I often do: a cup of tea, reading, and journaling. On this day, the tea and caffeine energized me, and I wrote in my journal that "I am feeling ready to tackle the day."

But then I stopped and looked at what I'd written.

Tackle the day.

What did the day ever do to deserve such treatment?

Consider the words we use to celebrate an accomplishment. People regularly congratulate one another for "crushing it" and "killing it." If you'd hunted a deer to feed your family, that would make sense. And metaphorically, I get it. There are obstacles to be overcome, challenges to defeat, and tasks demanding your inner warrior.

But when the day is an enemy to be tackled, crushed, or knocked out, that limits our options. It's also a recipe for frustration. If I seize the day, taking hold of it with the intent of bending it to my will, I can only be disappointed when that squirrely day squirms out of my grip and does something unexpected (as days are prone to do).

What if, instead of violenting the day, we tried to expand the day? Appreciate the day? Explore the day? Each intention creates a different opportunity and way to experience all that happens. If you've been a seizer of days, consider approaching your day differently and see what happens.

You might:

- Experience the day
- Savor the day
- Invest in the day
- Govern the day
- Love the day
- Flow the day
- Inhabit the day
- Embody the day
- Be the day
- Relish the day
- Connect to the day
- Live with zest today
- Nourish the day
- Raise the day
- Elevate the day
- Level up the day
- Discover the day
- Understand the day
- Comprehend the day
- Live the day
- Enjoy the day
- Dance with the day
- Jump with the day
- Twirl with the day
- Drink in the day
- Consume the day
- Embrace the day
- Hug the day
- Race the day

- Dive into the day
- Ride the day
- Explore the day
- Taste the day
- Smell the day
- Release the day

How will you approach today?

WHAT ARE YOU LOOKING FOR?

"In the same field the farmer will notice the crop, the geologists
the fossils, botanists the flowers, artists the colouring,
sportmen the cover for the game. Though we may all
look at the same things, it does not all follow
that we should see them."
—John Lubbock, *The Beauties of Nature and the Wonders
of the World We Live In*

Have you ever looked for something in your refrigerator or book-shelf and been unable to find it, only to later discover it was right there in front of you the whole time?

Often, this is because you went to the bookshelf looking for that blue paperback ... when in reality, the book was green. Or you opened the fridge searching for the metal bowl wrapped in foil, but those delicious leftovers were actually hiding in a Ziploc bag.

As frustrating as it is, there might be a reason your brain works this way.

A biologist looking at birds' eating patterns noticed something interesting. Imagine you're a bird that eats both worms and grass-hoppers. When there are equal amounts of worms and grasshoppers around, you might guess that you'd eat equal amounts of both—and you would be right.

But what happens when the availability of your food changes? Let's say there are now 70 percent grasshoppers and 30 percent worms available. You might guess that your diet would now reflect 70/30 grasshoppers to worms. But that's where it gets interesting—the birds actually ate *way* more grasshoppers. When grasshoppers are more prevalent, the birds almost stop eating worms and just eat grasshoppers. And it worked the other way too. Seventy percent worms available? The birds would almost ignore the grasshoppers in favor of worms. How curious! (Scientists love these moments of "well, that's weird"—it means there's a discovery about to happen.)

It turns out that when one source of food is more abundant, the birds' attention narrows to focus on just that one kind of food. When they're focused on grasshoppers, they don't see the worms, even though they could happily eat the worms. But why?

The answer is energy. When grasshoppers are more available, it takes fewer bird brain cells firing to focus on the insects. They get more food and spend less energy to find and catch it. That *search image* is an efficient way to stay alive and feed your baby birds.

In Los Angeles, you can find a strange sort of sign tied to telephone poles and fences or stuck in traffic cones. They usually feature a random word or group of letters placed over an arrow. They're also temporary, appearing and disappearing from day to day. These signs are production placards. They guide the cast and crew to filming locations without having to rely on maps or GPS. The random word or letters are code for a particular movie. With tight production schedules and multiple filming locations, the signs make it easy for everyone to get where they need to be. No addresses to worry about; just follow the signs with your codeword.

The production placards are bright yellow with black lettering— but there is no policy manual that mandates their color. A studio once asked for their placards to be made with a blue background and white lettering. The manufacturer printed three hundred of those blue signs, but within three days, the client returned and asked for the traditional yellow signs. Everyone was driving past the blue signs without seeing them.

That's search image—just like worms and grasshoppers.

In the 1990s, I served as an elected councilman for the city of Glendale, Colorado. One year, the council and the city staff started working on a plan to build the city's first preschool and kindergarten. At that point, there wasn't a single public preschool or kindergarten in the city. Families that wanted their children to attend these early education opportunities would bus or drive their students several miles, and our poorest kids were losing out on all the long-term learning gains that preschool was proven to offer.

But we were stuck.

Why? Well, in council meetings, people would offer an idea for moving the project forward, and it would get shot down. Bring up an idea for funding, and you'd get obstacles. Talk about features and design, and we'd immediately have three or four dissenting ideas. After weeks of this, Glendale's mayor, Joe Rice, stood up right in the middle of someone's this-won't-work speech about using the classrooms after school hours and made a timeout signal like a football referee.

He said, "We can find a thousand reasons why this won't work. But that's the wrong question. For the next ten minutes, let's share only about how we can make it work."

And in that moment, the mood shifted. The next person who spoke said, "If we can't afford to hold an after-school program for all the kids, as the last speaker said, then I'd like to make a plan for which ones we can serve. I propose that our first priority be to start with the youngest children—the four- and five-year-olds."

Energy built as the next speaker agreed and proposed holding a study session for their parents during the same period. That discussion continued for the rest of the meeting, and not one person mentioned going back to the old way of working on the project. Of course, some ideas didn't make the cut, but they didn't get in the way of the rest of the project moving forward. For many years now, the Glendale Early Childhood Education Center has given students who need it most a fantastic start on learning.

"How can we make it work?"

That's a question from a leader who understands the power of search image. Look for problems, and that's what you'll find. Look for beauty, and there it is. Look for solutions, and they'll appear.

What are you looking for?

DRY SHOES

"Knowledge is knowing that a tomato is a fruit;
wisdom is not putting it in a fruit salad."
–Miles Kington

Two boys walked home after a heavy rain. They'd just received new shoes.

Before they left home, their mother had given them very strict instructions not to ruin their new shoes in the water and mud.

Both boys tried very hard to do what their mother asked, but when they arrived home, one boy's shoes were muddy and soaking wet, while the other boy's shoes were dry. Naturally, the mother questioned her sons.

How did they manage to both walk the same route, both take her instructions seriously, and yet arrive home with such different results?

The brother with wet shoes answered, "I don't know, Mom, I tried to avoid all the puddles."

The brother with the dry shoes answered, "I looked for the dry places, and I put my feet there."

I imagine those two boys, one of them jumping back and forth, reacting to every puddle, trying to avoid them, but splashing in the edges despite his best efforts, while his brother calmly ignored the puddles and stepped only on dry patches of sidewalk.

A childhood mentor shared this story with me, and it's one I've recalled many times. When I'm most reactive and out of balance, it usually turns out I'm focused on avoiding what I don't want but haven't clarified what I *do* want.

Often, the difference between confusion and clarity is simply to change focus from what you don't want to what you do want. It's the difference between "I don't want to get my feet wet" versus "I want to keep my feet dry." Each of those desires creates very different activities.

What do you want?

POCO A POCO

"May your trails be crooked, winding, lonesome, dangerous,
leading to the most amazing view. May your
mountains rise into and above the clouds."
—Edward Abbey, *Desert Solitaire*

I fell asleep at 1:00 a.m., sandwiched between strangers and my daughter.

We were in a tent, the strangers on my right. They were a nice couple from Brazil—or at least whatever they said in Portuguese sounded nice. They smiled when they said it. All four of us cocooned in borrowed sleeping bags below the summit of Acatenango—the third tallest volcano in Central America.

After she finished college, my daughter, Averie, moved to Guatemala, where she founded a socially conscious clothing and textile production company. When I was able to take a week to visit her, she thoughtfully said, "Hey, you like hiking—there's a big dormant volcano here. We should hike up it."

I'm always up for a hike and a good time with my children, so I said sure. She signed us up, then emailed back with the details: Oh, this isn't a day hike. It's an overnight, guided backpacking experience with lots of medical forms and liability waivers.

A chance to follow the music?

And that's how I found myself on the side of a Central American volcano.

We'd spent the day trudging up the volcano, burdened with backpacks that were a function of our bodyweight. The heavier you are, the heavier your backpack. Mine weighed fifty pounds. (It's a cruel irony to give a guy who already had more weight to carry a heavier backpack–like some kind of reality-TV-inspired weight-loss incentive program.) I was also older than everyone else in our group by ten years. I asked if there was a backpack-weight reduction based on age–they just laughed.

We spent the day climbing through ash-enriched fields of coffee, flowers, and avocados, through a cloud rainforest, and into a dry ghost-forest of ash-choked trees killed by some old eruption. We set up camp one thousand feet below the summit. The plan was to get a good night's sleep, get up early, and reach the summit in time for a beautiful sunrise.

I thought sleep would come easily after the day's work, but it was not the case. Somehow my body was exhausted, but I couldn't fall asleep. The Brazilian couple had no such problem and were asleep in minutes.

Three hours after sleep finally came, a bright light shone through the window of the tent, and a gruff voice called out, "It's time to go." By 4:30 a.m., Averie and I were hiking up a steep incline, in the dark, on a crumbling trail through foot-deep sand. Each step up was a torturous effort to find a foothold before you slid back down the sandy slope. Oh, and I'd left my flashlight in the tent.

We hiked up that steep sandy slope for two hours.

Despite the many mountains I've hiked, this was the most grueling and mentally challenging ascent I'd ever done. While trails in the US use switchbacks to ease the pain of elevation gain and manage erosion, they haven't quite found their way into Guatemalan mountaineering yet. (Lack of sleep, and food that didn't agree with me, certainly didn't help!) And did I mention I was also older than everyone else in our group?

Have you ever found yourself in the middle of a difficult challenge with thoughts like:

> *What am I doing here?*
> *What was I thinking, believing I could do this?*
> *What if I can't make it?*

Every person who ever chooses to do or be something more or different than they are now will experience these doubts. They're part of the price you pay.

By 5:30 a.m., at 12,500 feet, Averie and I were alone. The younger, fitter group members (with lighter backpacks!) had gone on ahead. It was a different sort of alone than I'd experienced before—in a foreign country, nose clogged with dust, no idea how much farther we had to go or how difficult the trail would become. My daughter's small flashlight and a partial moon provided our only illumination in the dark.

Averie picked out the trail ahead of us. She would stop, shine her light, and look for the footprints of people who had climbed up the sandy trail before us. Then we would scramble up another twenty or thirty feet.

Stop. Catch our breath. Do it again.

Averie also hadn't slept well and was feeling lousy at this point. (Apparently, I snore. But the Brazilian couple slept through it, just saying ...) She told me I should go ahead and she'd catch up, or not, but she hurt. "No way," I said, "we're in this together." Every few minutes, I'd try to encourage her and lift her spirits.

When she'd had enough of that, she said, "Stop talking to me."

"Hey, this was your idea!"

"Don't remind me."

We trudged on in silence for a while, our spirits flagging.

That's when a guide from another group caught up to us. He was Guatemalan and accustomed to trekking up and down these mountains. As he passed us, he smiled, waved his hand in a huge cheery arc of greeting completely at odds with the expressions on our faces, and said, "Poco *a poco.*" Then he was gone, his smile and zero-percent-body-fat legs floating over the mountain like it was nothing.

Poco a poco.

That's "little by little" or, as I translate it, "one step at a time."

I often think of his "poco a poco."

Whatever challenge you face, poco a poco will help: look at the path immediately in front of you, find the tracks of the people who have gone before you, and take the next few steps. You don't have to know all the answers. You don't have to know how everything will turn out. You don't have to know how to do everything you'll be called upon to do.

I don't suggest that the work will be easy. Averie and I didn't talk to each other for an hour or more while we labored up the rim of Acatenango. At times the trail was so steep that I would literally take three steps, secure my footing, and stop to breathe.

But we made it. And so will you.

One thing I can promise: the view is worth the work to get there. This was easily the most spectacular sunrise I have ever seen in my life: a blanket of clouds below us, enveloping the cloud rainforest. Volcanoes poked through the clouds, some of them in the distance spewing ash and smoke from ongoing eruptions.

The journey will change you. You'll know you've done it—and can do it again.

Poco a poco.

WHERE THERE'S LIFE

"The question ... is not whether you will love, hurt, dream, and die.
It is what you will love, why you will hurt, when you
will dream, and how you will die. This is your choice.
You cannot pick the destination, only the path."
–Brandon Sanderson, *Oathbringer*

Two frogs fell into a barrel of milk just before someone placed a lid on it.

"Wait just a minute," you're probably saying. "Stop right there ... why was there a barrel of milk? Where did these frogs come from? And how did they fall into the barrel in the first place?"

Fair questions.

But this is the beginning of a story I heard as a child. And the thing about this kind of childhood story is that everything seems plausible. I'd never even seen a barrel of milk. Did that matter? Heck no ... there were two frogs in a barrel of milk; that's all we need to know. Now, back to the frogs ...

Faced with impending doom in this barrel of milk, the two frogs treaded water–or, uh, milk. Eventually, one of the frogs lost hope. "We'll never get out of here," the frog said. It stopped swimming and drowned.

The second frog (perhaps a devotee of *Finding Nemo's* Dory) just kept swimming, eventually churning the milk enough to produce a lump of butter. It rested on the floating lump of butter until someone removed the lid. Out it hopped and (we assume) lived happily ever after.

Okay, so it must have been a barrel of cream if the frog could churn it into butter. But that's not the point. The moral of the story, as I heard it, was, "Where there's life, there's hope."

As a teenager, I discovered that my friend Matt had heard the same story as a child but that he'd picked up a different take on the wisdom to be gleaned from these frogs. His takeaway: "If you're too dumb to give up, you might just make it."

We argued endlessly about the moral of the story (but never once about the veracity of frogs in a barrel of milk or cream). "Where there's life, there's hope" versus "If you're too dumb to give up, you might just make it."

There is a special kind of magic in persistence. To keep showing up and putting in the time and effort when your body doesn't want to, when it feels useless. When the critical voices nag, "Why bother? What difference will it make?"

There are times when you show up and do the work because you've trained yourself to persevere, to push through. Because you know the work is worth doing, even though the sun is obscured by clouds and you don't know which way is north. There is beauty and dignity in standing up and taking that next step ... because. That's Captain America at the end of Avengers: Endgame. Sure, it looks hopeless, but the universe rallies around those who stand up and take a step forward.

How would my life be different if I hadn't finished that pea project in high school? If I hadn't finished my first book? If I hadn't taken care of my sister as she finished high school and started college? If I hadn't run for city council and seen it through to the election? One single surrender to the despondent "why bother" would have stopped all that came after. So much of my life today hinged on the persistence to keep going that I must wonder: What is at stake that I'm no more aware of now than I was of the future each of those past decisions would reveal?

As a writer, I call this "butt glue" (the secret of writing is to glue your butt to the chair and write). I'm doing that now as I write these words. Choosing persistence and hope over the crushing clouds that whisper "why bother?" In the The War of Art, Steven Pressfield famously describes the act of showing up each day as an act of courage in the ongoing war against "Resistance"–the personification of everything that would keep you from your own mission, work, and what really matters. It's a superpower that's been described in so many ways.

"The only way out is through." I've seen these words ascribed to Akka Mahadevi–she was a twelfth century poet from India–along with certain translations of Dante's *Inferno*, a paraphrase of Shakespeare's Macbeth, and Robert Frost's poem "Servant to Servant." Then there's the popular wisdom often misattributed to Winston Churchill: "When you're going through hell, keep going."

Morgan Freeman purportedly tells his kids, "If you keep going, someone will always, always give you a hand. Always. But you gotta keep dancing, you gotta keep your feet moving."

Then there is Confucius's take: "It does not matter how slowly you go so long as you do not stop" (a mantra I've repeated many times during long runs, hikes, or interminable projects).

But my favorite expression of this truth is "where there's life, there's hope." Or maybe, "If you're too dumb to give up, you might just make it." I was partial to the optimistic version, but these days, I find truth in both (though I've still never seen a barrel of milk).

GOOD ENOUGH

"If it falls your lot to be a street sweeper, sweep streets
like Michelangelo painted pictures."
—Dr. Martin Luther King Jr.

Growing up, I internalized some really bad advice. You might have done the same. The problematic wisdom took many forms:

- The Cub Scout motto: "Do your best!"
- Every motivational poster or coach who encouraged us to "Give 110 percent!"
- At church, it was in the Bible's Old Testament book of Ecclesiastes: "Whatsoever thy hand findeth to do, do it with thy might; for there is no work, nor device, nor knowledge, nor wisdom, in the grave, whither thou goest."
- The New Testament got in on the action, too, in 1 Corinthians: "Whatever you do, do it all for the glory of God."
- In a speech to junior high school students, Dr. Martin Luther King Jr. added an awesome rhetorical flourish: "Don't just set out to do a good job. Set out to do such a good job that the living, the dead or the unborn couldn't do it any better. If it falls your lot to be a street sweeper, sweep streets like Michelangelo painted pictures, sweep streets like Beethoven composed music."

Do your best, give it 110 percent, do everything with all you have ... well, at the risk of contradicting thousands of years of wisdom, I've got to say: that's bad advice.

For one thing, it's just bad math. Here's the problem. Let's say I have a hundred kumquats (if you've never tried a kumquat, they're tasty little citrus fruits that you can eat whole—peel and all).

Now, if I give you 50 percent of my kumquats, how many do you have?

Right—you have fifty.

If I give you 100 percent of my kumquats, how many do you have?

One hundred—exactly. (I promise the math doesn't get any harder.)

But here's the tricky part. How do I give you 110 percent of my kumquats?

I can't—once I give you a hundred, that's all of them. The only way to give you 110 percent of my kumquats would be to borrow some. If I'm giving 110 percent of my effort, where would that extra effort come from?

But the motivational math gets worse. Think about what it means to give 100 percent. One hundred percent is everything. You can't possibly give another single ounce of energy ... you know what we call that?

Dead.

You'll know you really gave it 100 percent when it kills you—and I don't think that's what all those coaches, posters, or God had in mind. I'm thinking they'd probably be satisfied with 25 or 30 percent, tops.

Enough math ... what about "Do your best"?

Have you ever had a childhood dream that you continued to pursue as an adult?

I did.

For me, it was the dream of being a master-level chess player. Something only twenty thousand people in the world can claim to be.

Through high school and college, I played recreational but challenging chess. I read books on tactics, I joined chess clubs, and I went to tournaments for fun, sitting there for hours watching two guys hunched over a board. Then about the same time I got married ... I got serious about my dream.

I was going to do my best. I started a serious course of study. One that, with hard work and determination, would get me to my goal.

I stayed up nights solving problems where you had to think twelve to fifteen moves ahead.

I entered the chess tournaments. I played against masters and grandmasters. I did my best ... and it showed. After several months, I got better.

But in doing my best at chess, I realized that I was not doing my best in other areas of my life. For some reason, my wife and daughter weren't thrilled about coming to chess tournaments, and I was missing out on my life with them. Doing my best at chess meant not doing my best as a husband or a father.

I had a decision to make: I could not do my best at both. I had to choose where I would be the best. I chose my family and moved chess back to recreation. Because you can only be the best at a few things.

At times, the smart choice is to stop. To let a project go. To understand conditions aren't what you thought they were. Or the reward isn't worth the cost. There is wisdom in stopping so you can focus on what matters most.

For everything else ... good enough is good enough.

THE SAME SONG TWICE

"I want to be on the frontier."
–Bruce Springsteen

On the podcast *Conan O'Brien Needs a Friend*, I heard the comedian interview Bruce Springsteen. The Boss, who is known for the incredible energy he and the E Street Band bring to every performance, talked about his approach to performance. "I want to be on the frontier–on the edges of my own psychological, emotional spiritual frontier. I want to be working there until the day I die." That, Springsteen says, is what characterizes a professional. As you move forward and live life, he says, your life blossoms, so you can never actually sing the same song twice. You're always a new and different person.

The interview called to mind the first and only time I saw the band Kansas perform live. They were opening for the band Yes. This was decades after both bands' heyday. But you wouldn't have known it.

Kansas has two or three songs most rock fans know. They've probably performed that catalog thousands of times in venues ranging from huge stadiums in the 1970s to tents at state fairs.

When I saw them, it was in a smaller theater where I was standing in the back. And ...

They. Brought. It.

To this day, that opening act is one of the most energetic performances I've ever seen. The same few songs. "Dust in the Wind"—sung with the passion and perspective of people who have lived and seen life. "Carry On My Wayward Son"—filled with conviction, wisdom, and hope. "Point of Know Return"—carried passion, a challenge of adventure, and even an invitation to leadership.

They gave everything they had, and I'll never forget it.

What must it be like performing those same few songs over and over across decades? Their performance challenged me to show up for what matters most with all the energy and passion I can bring. To find what is new and fresh and meaningful.

JUST MAINTAINING

"Our very idea of productivity is premised on the idea of
producing something new, whereas we do not tend to see
maintenance and care as productive in the same way."
—Jenny Odell, *How to Do Nothing:
Resisting the Attention Economy*

As I'm writing, the political leaders of the United States are nego-
tiating (which might be a generous characterization) a large infrastructure bill. To generalize, one side takes the position that infrastructure includes things like roads, bridges, ports, transit systems,
and the electric grid. The other position takes a broader approach
and includes items like health care, technology, jobs training, and sci-
entific research in their definition of infrastructure. And yes, there
is much more nuance in the arguments from both perspectives, but
what's important here is that there's even a discussion about infrastructure. Both parties agree that they need to invest in infrastructure. The questions aren't "if," they are "what, where, and how much?"

My question is: Why?

Why do we need to have a conversation about maintaining our
infrastructure? When you build a road, you know it will deteriorate.

When you build a bridge, the engineers tell you upfront what the serviceable life of the bridge will be (and there are fun graphs that show the downward curve of the bridge's reliability over time). It's not a surprise—not in the way that the need for internet access grew over the past twenty years. So why aren't these costs planned for and incorporated as a normal, regular part of civic business?

The answer, in short, is that we don't value maintenance.

And yes, I recognize that there are many individual citizens, towns, states, and countries that do a wonderful job planning and maintaining their infrastructure. I'm speaking culturally. In the US, we emphasize the new, the forward, and put little focus, energy, or value in keeping things going, alive, healthy, and whole. Continual forward-focus is a problem for our country as we look at deteriorating infrastructure. It's a problem for our budgeting when we save for the house or the car but don't plan for the maintenance costs. Looking for the new at the cost of maintenance is also a problem for relationships.

There's a cultural negativity associated with maintaining.

If you're "just" maintaining, you're confessing to underperforming, being a slacker, treading water, going nowhere. Our maintenance workers are arguably some of the most vital people to continue our way of life and the comforts we take for granted. But maintenance work doesn't get a cultural spotlight. Those jobs aren't portrayed as shiny and meaningful in popular culture. Because these jobs don't uncover, explore, or discover what's new.

Early in my career, I worked for a human service organization whose leader had a strong disdain for maintenance. Maintaining didn't feel like building the future. He framed our work in terms of warfare. "You don't see soldiers storming the beaches at Normandy stopping and taking care of the injured," he told me. "Neither can we! We've got to take ground and keep moving forward."

I still cringe when I replay those words. His values and vision focused entirely on the new and shiny—at the cost of caring for the organization he'd built and the people who were a part of it. You can imagine the culture of chaos. Maintenance, in his view, wouldn't build the future.

And yet ... maintaining gets us *to the future.*

I love baking bread the slow, natural artisan way. Feed and maintain the starter (a mixture of flour, water, yeast, and bacteria). Let it sit until it triples in size, then mix it with flour, water, and a little salt. Give it time. Knead it or fold it over the course of three or four hours. Feel the dough come together as the yeast multiply and proteins in the flour align and connect.

Shape the dough a final time and put it in a proofing basket. And give it more time—even overnight in the refrigerator before baking. While it bakes, the aroma tempts you to cut into a freshly baked loaf, but even then, you're better to wait a little longer and let the interior cool down and fully develop.

There is much maintenance in this bread. The starter is maintained. The dough is tended and maintained. The bread itself feeds, nurtures, and maintains my family and friends.

Cooking for family and friends brings me joy. And it is maintenance. Literal life and connection and joy and energy are in fueling and caring for one another. You maintain a friendship by investing in it. You maintain a car with regular service. Maintain a culture. Maintain your health. Maintain your relationships. These acts of maintenance get you to your future in a healthy way so you can do something meaningful.

Life isn't only maintenance—there is a yin-yang energy integration at work here. To build your body's strength, you need the energy of both movement and recovery, of running and resting. One without the other leads to illness or injury. So it is with maintenance.

And for the yang-filled, high-energy explorers, builders, and creators who still find maintenance challenging, I'll leave you with this thought from Robert Ludlum's Jason Bourne series: "Sleep is a weapon."

INTERLUDE IV

SNOWY FOREST

"I wonder if the snow loves the trees and fields,
that it kisses them so gently? And then it covers
them up snug, you know, with a white quilt;
and perhaps it says, 'Go to sleep, darlings,
till the summer comes again.'"
—Lewis Carroll, *Alice's Adventures in Wonderland*

I walk in twice-reflected sunlight—once from the moon and once from the snow.

The air is thick with icy crystals, the cold condenses the humidity and freezes it, and the ice hangs in the air, spiking and needling as I walk.

But the sensation is friendly, welcoming. The air-alive calls me forward to pause and listen. To hear the rhythms and wind and deep resting of the trees. The silence of the forest, waiting, reserving its strength, in a deep slumber. Restoring itself.

And though asleep, full of life. The whisper-soft thump of a rabbit breaking through the top crust of snow on its way to its den. The creak and crash of a branch whose time was up as its tree releases it, and the branch falls through the canopy to the forest floor. The fallen branch hangs on a lower limb, balanced for one moment before tipping off and landing with a crack at the foot of the tree. I look around and see my tracks behind me.

When I move, I crunch the snow, and the sound deafens but does not overwhelm. Snow covers the trees, ground, and rocks; muffles, absorbs; and there is peace.

SECTION V

THE MOUNTAIN
ALWAYS WINS

"What are men to rocks and mountains?"
—Jane Austen, *Pride and Prejudice*

At Let's Grow Leaders, we talk a lot about confidence and humility. The most effective leaders combine these characteristics. They have the confidence to say, "Together, we can have a better future. Together, we can do something bigger than ourselves." They also have the humility to acknowledge their limitations, admit when they're wrong, ask for help, and invite opinions that differ from their own.

For me, there is no better teacher of confidence and humility than nature. When I speak of nature, I mean the mountains. Specifically, the Colorado Rocky Mountains. We are all from somewhere or, for some of us, somewheres. I embrace bioregionalism—the notion that we are citizens, not just of a body politic, but of a place. An ecosystem. For you, the great teacher might be the desert, the ocean, the prairie, or the streets of a large metropolis. For me, no matter where I might call home, the ecology and places that shaped me are the Rocky Mountains and the Great Plains of Colorado. Growing up in the shadow of these peaks, exploring their mysteries, challenging myself on their trails, I became me. There is nowhere I am more at home.

It takes confidence to set foot on their slopes. Without confidence, you cannot hope to explore and experience their beauty, awe, and wonder. But if you do not approach the mountains with humility, they can kill you. In this section, you will find reflections on the power of humility, ways to build your confidence, the role of nature in our lives, and what it means to be alive.

THE MOUNTAIN
ALWAYS WINS II

"The hard facts were a lot more helpful than a happy lie."
—Christopher McDougall, *Running with Sherman*

What's the difference between confidence and arrogance?

A mountain trail gave me an early lesson between the two. It was Labor Day weekend my freshman year of high school, and my friend Mike asked if I wanted to hike a "fourteener" with him.

In Colorado, "fourteener" or "14er" refers to the tallest mountain peaks—those that rise above fourteen thousand feet. The state boasts fifty-three of these peaks (fifty-eight if you use the most generous definition). Hiking them is a pastime for many Colorado outdoor enthusiasts, but up to that point in my life, I had yet to do it.

A key feature of hiking these peaks is that you start early. Like, you get up at 4 a.m., drive, grab breakfast, and arrive at the trailhead by 6 a.m. or earlier. You start early to get up and down the mountain before afternoon lightning storms.

I waited in the dark outside my house for Mike and his mom to pick me up. I wore brand-new hiking boots and a pair of blue floral print shorts my mom had sewn for me. We arrived at the Mount Bierstadt trailhead and started hiking just before sunrise. Crusts of ice

138

lined the edge of the mountain stream, and icy dewdrops weighed down the willow branches.

Oh, the willows. The trail winds through acres of shrubby willow bogs before climbing up the stony peak. The soil in these bogs was wet and soft in places, a tenuous mat of decayed branches that held you up like a suspension bridge above icy dark willow juice.

In the middle of the trail, we encountered a churned-up, muddy stretch. It looked like the muck would be soft and slimy during the day, but right now, the frosty mountain morning had frozen the mud. The dark ice looked cold and solid. Nevertheless, Mike, his mom, and our friend Matt walked around the mud.

I, however, had new boots. Strong boots. Boots that wouldn't mind a little muck. After all, isn't that what boots are made for? And so, I boldly stepped on the ice-encrusted mud.

And sank up to my waist.

My friends tried to pull me out, but the cold, wet slime created a vacuum. As they pulled, I could feel my feet sliding out of my boots. Ultimately, my friends found several long branches that we were able to wedge down by my feet and work around, moving aside enough mud that it released the vacuum that had threatened to steal my once-proud boots.

When my friends hauled me out of the mud, my hand-sewn blue floral shorts weren't blue anymore. By the end of the day, the dried crusty mud covering my legs, infiltrating my socks, and chafing between my toes was the start of a valuable lesson.

The mountain always wins.

It's a lesson I would learn more deeply as I became familiar with these peaks.

I mentioned that you start early so that you're well off the summit by noon. That's when the lightning storms begin. These storms come up suddenly because the sun warms the exposed rocky peaks. That heat radiates from the stones into the surrounding atmosphere, which warms and rises in a column. The rising mass meets cooler air above it. As the rising air cools, moisture condenses, forming clouds. All this energy and moving air creates electricity.

One time I was on my way down the mountain well before noon but not before electrified clouds swirled up and sleet pelted us. Women with longer hair found it standing straight up. I hike with collapsible metal walking poles, and as I swung the pole forward, the air around it audibly crackled with energy. People stopped for pictures—but that's a good way to get killed. We ran down the mountain and were lucky. (Lightning kills an average of eleven people each year in Colorado's mountains.)

The mountain always wins.

You may have prepared for an ascent for months and hiked for the better part of a day, but a storm comes up. There's only one healthy choice: turn around.

There's a difference between the grit of confident resiliency and arrogance. Grit, confidence, and resiliency help us to push through our self-imposed barriers, to understand our potential, and to stand on heights we may never have imagined. But arrogance is a failure to understand ourselves and our environment, to confront the hard facts. Arrogance embraces McDougall's "happy lie."

I love the mountains because they are such potent teachers. They draw out grit, build confidence, and reward resiliency, but you cannot cheat the mountain.

The mountain always wins.

A BEAUTIFUL QUESTION

"You can tell whether a man is clever by his answers.
You can tell whether a man is wise by his questions."
–Naguib Mahfouz

A bird sings outside my window.

A cardinal. It starts early, before the sun is up.

Is he singing or boasting or calling for attention or serenading the new day? Or is he looking for a mate and proving his prowess? What's interesting is that on some days, his singing is ebullient, a celebration of life. But on other days, his notes are intrusive, annoying, painful as they pierce my groggy consciousness, demanding attention. What has changed between the two songs? Certainly, he's not singing any differently.

Sunlight can feel the same way. One day the sun is a warming friend. Bringing my skin and body to life, filling me with Vitamin D, and nourishing my soul. And then there are the days where the sun strikes without mercy. Harsh, glaring, oppressive, and relentless. Driving me to shade or indoors. It's the same sun. What's different? I'm sure weather patterns are involved. The tilt of the Earth. The time of year. The presence or absence of clouds. The temperature. But with all these differences, it's still the same sun. How can I greet it with welcoming joy one day and hostility the next?

On a winter hike with my friend Kevin, we stopped and turned to watch the snow falling, filling a beautiful ice-encrusted valley. The wind blew, the snow collected in the crevices around our eyes, and it covered everything in a calm white blanket. We soaked in the quiet beauty, enjoying the solitude and peace, the experience made richer knowing that someone else shared the moment. After enough time passed, Kevin said, "Does it ever amaze you that the same nature that we find so beautiful and comforting in this moment can, at the same time, be haunting, menacing, and deadly?"

It's a beautiful question.

And my answer is yes, it is amazing.

I'd been contemplating the same truth when he voiced his thoughts. Is the winter valley peaceful and restorative? Menacing with grave portent? Hostile and repelling? Inviting, like an old friend?

Nature is all of these. The valley's powerful winter storm nourished us and brought peace and connection. But in a brief moment, the experience could change ... a slip, a fall, a wrong turn, and it might be a deadly beauty. The same valley, the same storm.

The cardinal, the sun, the snow—all the same.

But I am different.

I make the cardinal encouraging or intrusive. My perception changes the sun from nourishing to aggressive. My preparedness invites the snow or perishes in it. I receive what the world has to give me through the lens of my emotions, experiences, and whims. Nature is neutral—it grows and dies and sings and decays indifferent to you. It is both friend and foe, distinct from and a part of you. But what nature is in each moment depends on who you are when you arrive. So it is with all of life.

I am different, and I change.

And if I change from day to day—can I choose my filters? Can I welcome the hostile sun for the good it does, even if I don't feel it in that moment? Can I thank the cardinal for its song, even when my fuzzy brain would rather rest?

LAZY RIVER

"You never change things by fighting the existing reality.
To change something, build a new model that makes
the existing model obsolete."
—R. Buckminster Fuller

I fell backward off the side of a boat and descended into the Pacific Ocean. I was about to get another incredible lesson —and not from a mountain this time.

I'm a relatively new scuba diver and was diving with my family in the Galapagos Islands. This would be my first current dive. A current dive is where you drop into the ocean and swim along with the current. You don't have to swim back to the boat; it picks you up at the end of the dive.

The Divemaster reviewed the plan, we put on our wetsuits and gear, and then we rolled off the boat into the ocean. We grouped up twenty feet below the surface at a rocky ledge, then the Divemaster led us around the ledge and into the current.

It was at this point I realized how poorly I had misunderstood the word "current." I was thinking of a water park's Lazy River ride where you float along on an inflated tube, enjoying the scenery. This was something else entirely—like a dam had burst and swept up everything in its path.

Invisible. Irresistible.

I could swim to the left; I could swim to the right. I could swim up or down. What I could not do was turn around or go back. Even giving it my full physical effort, if I tried to swim against the current, I couldn't even stay in place and would exhaust my air in minutes.

Our guide signaled us to take it easy and let the water carry us—and the views were fantastic. So many ocean fish, sea turtles, and black-tipped sharks resting in sandy depressions, protected from the current as it carried us above them. And I wouldn't have seen any of it if I fought the current.

In my early twenties, I injured my back. I'd been horribly sore for weeks but decided to play volleyball anyway. I dove for a ball that was just out of reach—and I didn't get up.

I was born with my spine not quite aligned properly. A condition I exacerbated while roughhousing with friends and carrying heavy backpacks filled with schoolbooks (rather than stashing them in my locker—I was stubborn that way). When I dove for the volleyball, I ruptured a vertebra in my lower back that had been bulging for months.

For the next two months, I couldn't walk, could only sleep three or four hours a night due to the pain, and ultimately needed surgery.

As I recovered from the surgery, I found that I could not straighten my right leg or walk more than a block. My muscles had atrophied.

But I was way too young to spend the rest of my life like that. I wanted to hike again and enjoy life. So, I joined a gym and worked with a trainer to restore my strength and mobility.

Despite my motivation to get better, I struggled. In the winter months, the 5 a.m. alarm waking me up to hit the gym before work ran into the reality of icy cold, dark mornings, lingering pain, and a little self-pity. Far too often, I hit the snooze button.

Things finally changed when I made one small adjustment. In the evening as I prepared for bed, I would pick out all my work clothes—

everything—and put them, along with my bath towel and shampoo, in the car.

My evening self was more than happy to do that; it was easy and didn't take much effort at all. But now my morning self woke up to an entirely different environment—the clothes I needed for work, along with the towel and shampoo I needed to shower, were all in the car. If I wanted to get dressed for work, I had to go to the car. And if I made it to the car, well, now I was already cold and in the car ... I might as well go on to the gym. Karin told me that she and her sister also used this technique when they were young. They'd go to sleep wearing their swimsuits so they could get up for early swim practice.

Loading my car was a small change to my environment, but it did the trick—within ten months of that surgery, I had rehabbed enough to hike up two fourteen-thousand-foot mountains.

Many forces in your life are like that ocean current. Invisible. Powerful. Inexorable. Fighting them is frustrating and saps your motivation. But the current can also carry you where you want to go.

Your environment is one of the most powerful "currents" in your life. Changing your environment is one of the fastest ways I know to overcome inertia and help create positive change. Your brain is always looking for shortcuts: What's the easiest thing to do, the way that will take the least amount of energy? (There's nothing wrong with you—it's a survival thing from back when energy from food was rare and precious.)

It can be hard to fight, but this hardwiring can work for you, too. Create your own current by changing your environment to make your new habit the easiest choice. Your environment might be physical, like putting my clothes and towel in the car. Or it may be social—surrounding yourself with people who are doing what you want to do. Your brain will take these cues. Eventually, the habit becomes your default "shortcut"—the powerful current that takes you where you want to go.

What currents carry you?

COLORADO SPRING

"Spring is the time of year when it is summer in the sun
and winter in the shade."
—Charles Dickens, *Great Expectations*

"Colorado doesn't have a real spring," my friend from Illinois griped while boasting of his gradually greening parks, gentle rains, and the burst of color that comes every April. "Everything here is snowy one day and green the next. You don't have a real spring. It goes straight from winter to summer."

I had to protest; he'd never spent enough time to savor a real Colorado spring—the kind that lasts for months.

The decades I lived in Colorado, my annual spring ritual began in February, playing hide-and-seek with tiny crocus poking through a thin blanket of snow in Front Range gardens. Their hardy, purple, snow-capped petals foretold the arrival of warmer weather and longer days.

But spring in Colorado is not a gentle affair. Like the mountains and plains, it is rugged—savage in its beauty, capable of drowning rains and instant blizzards that snow you in for days, Chinook winds (the Blackfoot people called these winds "snow eaters") that devour the drifts just as quickly, and streets that fill with rivers of running water.

Eventually, the snow recedes and trees blossom. Spring creeps up the hills.

That's the real magic of a Colorado spring—if you recognize spring by the receding of winter snow, then you can follow the season up the mountains all through June. Mountainsides flow with waves of fresh snowmelt in a delicious mix of freezing mud and alpine flowers soaking in icy baths. You can escape midsummer heat in the shadowed recesses of stony fourteen-thousand-foot mountains where spring might arrive for a brief week, just in time to herald the oncoming winter. For six months in Colorado, spring is only a short car trip away. If only my friend were so lucky.

OATMEAL AND SCOTCH

"The minute you get away from fundamentals—
whether it's proper technique, work ethic, or
mental preparation—the bottom can fall out
of your game, your schoolwork, your job,
whatever you're doing."
–Michael Jordan

Imagine that you're camping in the wilderness, many miles away from the nearest town or gas station. As you set up camp and go to sleep, what do you do with your food?

Even if you've never camped a day in your life, you likely know the answer. It's one of the first camping rules you learn: if your car is close, put it in the car. If you're backpacking, suspend it between two trees. And whatever you do, don't put food in your tent—that's how people get "attacked" by bears or other hungry critters.

I grew up camping and loved it. Leaving the city and daily cares behind for the beauty of running water, forests, and mountains. Of mysterious stories, and games played over square miles. The danger of getting lost and elation of finding my way back again. The mystery of a campfire, of ghost stories, cheese and crackers or s'mores or peach cobbler. Rising just before the sun and sitting quietly with a cup of steaming tea, listening and watching for animals that were either waking up or settling down for the day.

My daughter enjoyed it, too, and when she was sixteen, she invited her friend, Gabby, to come camping with us. Gabby and my daughter were co-captains of their high school basketball team—and Gabby had never been camping before in her life.

Awesome!

I leapt into super-camp-dad mode, excited for the chance to give Gabby a great first camping experience. We picked her up from her house on a sunny Friday morning, and spirits were high as we drove to the mountains, arrived at the campground early enough to pick out a favorite site, and set up camp.

The tent went up without a hitch, and I split wood for our evening campfire while the girls unloaded the sleeping bags from the car. We found a nice shady spot for the cooler underneath the picnic table, set up the camp stove and our water containers, and by 1:00 p.m., we'd set up a campsite worthy of the cover of *Outdoor Life*.

We ate lunch, explored the ponderosa pine forest and nearby river, then hopped in the car to drive to the top of a nearby pass. There are days in the mountains that are so crisp and beautiful you feel the view physically in your chest—this was one of those days. We followed the road down the other side of the mountain, passing crystal-clear beaver ponds, blue and white columbine flowers, and stunning panoramic views of a mountain valley. Called by the beauty, we continued our drive, found a little town with a fantastic coffee shop, and sipped our tea (me) and lattes (the girls) as we drove back to camp.

Gabby was loving the day, my daughter was enjoying Gabby's company, and I felt like super-camp-dad-level-10. Then we got back to camp.

Gabby ran ahead while I locked up the car. As I closed the door, I heard her shout with wonder, "A giant chipmunk's been in our camp!"

My heart fell. I didn't need to see it. As soon as she called out, I knew what had happened.

A) There's no such thing as a giant chipmunk. It had to be a bear.

B) Remember that cooler of food we'd put in the shade beneath the picnic table?

Yeah.

My daughter and I joined Gabby and surveyed the damage. The bear had dragged the cooler from beneath the table, pried it open, and eaten—everything. You could see the bite marks on the carton of milk. Shredded bits of plastic were all that remained of our bread and lunch meat. And not so much as a cherry pit or peel remained of our fruits and vegetables. It had eaten everything.

Well, not quite everything.

I'd put a bottle of scotch in the cooler. It was lying on the ground with three claw marks scratched down the label like some kind of ursine code telling me, "I didn't, but I could have."

We cleaned up the mess, grateful that the bear hadn't damaged our tent or other equipment.

Then it started to rain.

I dug around in the car and found some oatmeal packets we hadn't unloaded. The girls tried to put a good face on things, but as we huddled around our campfire in the rain eating our paltry dinner of oatmeal (the girls) and scotch (me), I felt like the end screen of The Oregon Trail video game. "A bear ate all your food and your children are starving. Please start over."

Ouch, back to camp-dad-level-1.

It was a lesson in fundamentals. Michael Jordan said it all: get away from fundamentals, for even a minute, and "the bottom can fall out." I hadn't respected the fundamentals, but the bear had. After all, you don't touch a person's scotch without permission.

POSTLUDE

I WAS HERE

"Life has a way of talking to the future. It's called memory."
—Richard Powers, *The Overstory*

You can see it from the road.

The image of a lizard chipped into the stone's desert varnish. It's nearly three feet long, twenty feet off the ground, and was created by the Fremont people over a thousand years ago. It probably took the artist(s) several months to complete.

Standing on a hot, windswept ledge in the Utah desert, many miles from the nearest person or car, looking at this ancient masterpiece, it's hard not to think about why.

Why is it there? What did the artist want to communicate? What does it have to say to us?

Most of these answers are lost in antiquity. We just don't know whether the image and so many petroglyphs like it have spiritual significance, were ancient hunting billboards, or were artistic displays meant to celebrate their subjects or the artist's ability. But one thing I do know: the artist was there.

Drive along Interstate 70 through western Kansas, and you'll see a sign pointing south to Monument Rocks Natural Landmark. It's worth the couple hours roundtrip out of your way to pay a visit. Huge spires of chalky white rock rise up to dominate the flat Kansas prairie. The rock in these pillars is soft and powdery; if you were to touch it with any force (which you shouldn't), it would crumble. These huge powdery rock formations survive because there are harder caps of rock on top of the softer rock. These harder rock caps act like geologic umbrellas, protecting the chalky rock below from the elements. At least for a while—one of the most recognizable formations collapsed in 1986, and the others will eventually erode away too. (The mountain always wins ... but even mountains bow to wind and rain.)

These towering white monuments were hunting grounds for native peoples. Then they were a significant point of reference for gold-seekers heading to Denver on the Smoky Hill Trail. In the later 1800s, soldiers occupied a fort just south of the spires. Nothing remains of the fort, but if you look carefully at the spires and the light is just right, you might find a soldier's etching in the rock. A name and date, a one-hundred-and-fifty-year-old, chalky-soft, half-eroded reminder that "I was here."

There is a bridge in nearly every major US city with a spray-painted tag that, when you stop to consider it, defies imagination. The artfully rendered pseudonyms blend into the urbanscape background. But look carefully and consider what gymnastics or feats of engineering it took to place that tag there. The hard-to-reach location is both a declaration of the artist's mastery as well as some guarantee of a longer lifespan. The pseudonym, designed to evade law enforcement, is still a declaration: I was here.

World War II saw one of the most viral "I was here" events the world has ever known. Ships and tanks and installations around the world featured a little round head, eyes, and fingers peering over the straight line of a wall, accompanied by the words "Kilroy was here." Throughout the 1940s, the image and words appeared around the world from Europe to Japan—even sparking angst in the intelligence arms of the Japanese and German militaries.

They needn't have feared.

The image started in a shipyard in Massachusetts. A rivet inspector named James J. Kilroy had a problem. He was paid by the number of rivets he inspected, but the normal way of recording your work was to make a chalk mark on the machinery. These marks were easily rubbed off, and the rivet line taken over by someone else. So, Kilroy began inscribing "Kilroy was here" along with the image. It wasn't easily erased, and he got paid for his work. But in the busy war effort, the ships often didn't get their final coats of paint and were sent to the front with Kilroy's mark in place—often in weird locations once everything was assembled.

From there, the image became a sort of good-luck charm for the US troops. Kilroy spread from the ships to anywhere the soldiers could conceivably draw him. Eventually, the symbol made its way to Mount Everest, the Great Wall of China, and even the surface of the moon. Kilroy might be the best "I was here" the world has ever known.

What is it that compels us to leave these marks?

It's easy to attribute the compulsion to our fear of death, of being forgotten. But that's too convenient and doesn't fit the facts. The petroglyph lizard is very cool but, along with every other petroglyph, has lost its original meaning. No one knows the people who made them. Graffiti tags use a pseudonym, and most people don't know and can't possibly remember the artist. Kilroy's originator didn't intend the sketch to last any longer than he needed to get paid—and the troops who duplicated it around the world used it anonymously as a meme.

Perhaps the motivation isn't to remind the future but to declare one's existence to the present. I *am* here. Or maybe there's nothing more to it than a bit of creative fun and artistry in the moment—to see what one's capable of doing without considering what people will think about it next week, much less next millennia.

In our research for our book *Courageous Cultures: How to Build Teams of Micro-Innovators, Problem Solvers, and Customer Advocates*, Karin and I asked survey participants: "If you have an idea or solution you could contribute to your organization, what would keep you from sharing it?"

The most common answer was "not getting credit for my idea."

This feels closer to the reason why people make their mark on the physical world.

See me. Know that I exist.

And yet, how many creations do you depend on every day without knowing a single bit of information about the person who invented them? Who designed your chair? Who invented the regulator that allows you to use natural gas or propane to cook? Who designed the font you're reading right now? The vaccines and medicines that have kept you alive? Your car? Your coffeemaker? We don't need to know in order to use them, but the creations survive and become part of how we live.

We survive in one another.

Every human breath is a declaration to the universe of the many generations that came before. They were here.

I do not know their names, but I have received their gifts, their creations, their love.

Know me and know them.

And when you see future generations, see my gifts, my love, and my creation in them.

What gifts, love, and creation will the future enjoy from you?

ENDNOTES

1. The Economist. 2021. "The Pandemic's True Death Toll." https://www.economist.com/graphic-detail/coronavirus-excess-deaths-estimates.

2. Newell, John Phillip. *Sacred Earth Sacred Soul*. HarperOne, 2021.

3. Chodron, Pema. *Comfortable with Uncertainty*. Shambhala, 2018.

4. Godin, Seth. 2021. "Tools for Modern Citizens." Seth's Blog. https://seths.blog/2021/10/tools-for-modern-citizens/.

5. Green, John. *The Anthropocene Reviewed: Essays on a Human-Centered Planet*. Penguin Random House, 2021.

6. Nhat Hanh, Thich. McLeod, Melvin, ed. *Your True Home*. Shambhala, 2011. p 42.

7. Ahmaud Arbery was an unarmed 25-year-old Black man who was jogging in Glynn County, Georgia. He was pursued and shot by three white men who followed him in two vehicles.

8. 1863 September 18, New York Herald, "The President's Habeas Corpus Proclamation and the Act of Congress on the Subject," Quote Page 6, Columns 4 and 5, New York.

9. As quoted in Brach, Tara. *Radical Compassion: Learning to Love Yourself and Your World with the Practice of RAIN*. 2019.

10. DeMello, Anthony. 2020, December 31. "The Finest Act of Love." Tony's Blog. https://www.demellospirituality.com/the-finest-act-of-love/.

11. ildan, Mehmet Murat [@ildanquotations]. "Tweet message." Twitter, February 19, 2021, https://twitter.com/ildanquotations/status/1362892932332847108.

12. Nouwen, Henri. *Bread for the Journey: A Daybook of Wisdom and Faith*. HarperCollins, 1997.

13. Glass, Ira. (2016, February 20). *Reinventing Radio: An Evening with Ira Glass*. Denver, Colorado, United States of America.

14. Quote Investigator. 2014, September 14. *If You're Going Through Hell, Keep Going*. https://quoteinvestigator.com/2014/09/14/keep-going/.

15. Western, Dan. 23 *Morgan Freeman Quotes That He Actually Said*. https://wealthygorilla.com/12-morgan-freeman-quotes-actually-said/ Accessed December 21, 2021.

16. King Jr., Martin Luther (1967, October 26). *What's Your Life's Blueprint?* [Speech video recording]. https://www.youtube.com/watch?v=202nbcLwxs-g&ab_channel=SingjuPost.

17. O'Brien, Conan, host. "#97 Bruce Springsteen." *Conan O'Brien Needs a Friend*, October 25, 2020. https://www.earwolf.com/episode/bruce-springsteen/.

18. The Nobel Prize [@NobelPrize]. "Tweet message." Twitter, December 11, 2019. https://twitter.com/nobelprize/status/1204660848515567616.

19. Fuller, R. Buckminster. Buckminster Fuller Institute. https://www.bfi.org/ideaindex/projects/2015/greenwave. Accessed December 28, 2021.

20. Whipps, Heather. "How 'Kilroy Was Here' Changed the World." LiveScience, September 15, 2008. https://www.livescience.com/7577-kilroy-changed-world.html.

ABOUT THE AUTHOR

David Dye helps human-centered leaders find clarity in uncertainty, drive innovation, and achieve breakthrough results. He's the President of Let's Grow Leaders, an international leadership development and training firm known for practical tools and leadership development programs that stick.

He's the award-winning author of several books including *Courageous Cultures: How to Build Teams of Micro-Innovators, Problem Solvers, and Customer Advocates* and *Winning Well: A Manager's Guide to Getting Results-Without Losing Your Soul* and hosts the popular *Leadership without Losing Your Soul* podcast.

David is a former executive and elected official. David and his wife and business partner, Karin Hurt, are committed to their philanthropic initiative, Winning Wells – building clean water wells for the people of Cambodia.